CU00728280

THE LITTLE GUIDE TO
YOUR
BIGGER
FUTURE™

Helping you towards a
healthier, wealthier,
happier and longer life

Brian G Morman

Sybil
Here's to your
bigger future
Brian x

THE LITTLE GUIDE TO YOUR BIGGER FUTURE ™

Copyright © 2017 by Brian G. Morman

The right of the author to be so identified has been asserted in accordance with the Copyright, Design and Patent Act 1988. All rights reserved. No part of this publication may be reproduced or transmitted in any form or by any means (electronic, mechanical or otherwise) without prior permission of the copyright holder except for brief quotations within critical articles and reviews.

Please note that the views expressed in this book are those of the author, having researched and listened to world experts. It seeks to provide information, insight and inspiration and is not intended as medical advice or a substitute for common sense or professional advice from your doctor, financial consultant or accountant, etc.

Edited and designed by D J Morman

 PREFACE

Why do we do the things we do? What makes us stretch ourselves beyond our normal, everyday activities? Why did I, at the age of 60, decide to write a book – this book?

The answer is simple. I felt I had a positive message that I could share with others, to help them have better lives.

The catalyst was in fact my 60th birthday. I set myself six challenges for the year (www.brian60.co.uk) to raise money for the local children's charity that has always been close to my heart – The Pied Piper Appeal. I wanted to help the charity refurbish the oncology playroom at their facility in Gloucester Royal Hospital.

With the help and support of family, friends and colleagues, I ran a half marathon, 'flew' down one of the longest and fastest zip wires in the world, climbed three mountains ('The Three Peaks Challenge'), managed a 'red run' on the Andorran ski slopes (having never skied before), and accomplished a wing walk. The sixth and final challenge was to write a book, with a proportion of any proceeds going to the charity.

So, "I'll write a book," I said. Easier said than done. What I thought would take a few months has occupied me for over two years. I take my hat off to authors. It really is very hard work! But what a fantastic and fascinating journey it has been. A learning curve, certainly, but I've also come to realise that I am not fearful for the future. I practice what I preach. I'm fitter, happier in myself and am always looking forward.

But where would I have been during the research and construction process without my wife Deb's valuable, down-to-earth input – and (often painful) – critique? And in my capacity as a full-time financial consultant, how would I have found time to sit down, write and design a book without my brother Dave taking on the infinitely frustrating job of being my 'ghost writer?'

There are just too many other people to thank personally for their inspiration, material, anecdotes and sheer good advice. I hope you know who you are and how grateful I am to you for your encouragement, love and support. Thank you all very much.

Wishing you a good, long, happy, healthy and wealthy life.

CONTENTS

I intend to live forever, or die trying

Groucho Marx
American comedian
and film star

1 INTRODUCTION

1 INTRODUCTION

Always make your future bigger than your past

Dan Sullivan
American visionary, innovator
and conceptual thinker

These are extraordinary times. The reality is that we are likely to live longer than our parents and grandparents - considerably longer if some sources are to be believed.

At the turn of the 20th century, a man could count himself lucky if he lived beyond the age of 50. Today, that expectation has risen to nearly 80. This is possibly one of society's greatest achievements. Some experts even believe that we are on the verge of semi-immortality, thanks to advances in medical research. Whether you are inclined to believe that or not, we are undoubtedly moving into exciting, uncharted territory.

That's good news, then. Well, yes of course, providing we can live each day to be healthy, happy and fulfilled. But on the surface, it raises more questions than answers. What does it actually mean? Does it mean our often unhealthy lifestyles will condemn us to spend longer in ill health as we age? Will we have enough money to sustain ourselves? Will we be able to cope with increasing information overload? Will we become confused, weighed down, unable to make clear decisions? How will we prepare for a longer life? In short, how will *you* prepare for a bigger future – Your Bigger Future ™?

In order to move forward positively, we need to have a clear vision of our respective futures, our children's futures and our grandchildren's futures. We need to prepare ourselves physically, mentally and financially for a longer life. And we need to be able to visualise our lives.

Why do I find this subject fascinating? As a financial consultant for more years now than I care to remember, I've met people from all walks of life and discussed with them their dreams for the future. It's been my privilege to play a small part in helping them make those aspirations become reality. I think I have one of the best jobs in the world!

I've listened to accounts about hardship, tragedy, good luck and love. I've heard stories that have genuinely inspired me. I've heard tales that are just the plain, every day. But almost without exception - and it doesn't matter whether I'm talking to a client of modest means or a millionaire - the two concerns uppermost in everyone's mind are:

A) WILL I STAY HEALTHY?
B) WILL MY MONEY LAST?

Perhaps they are high on your list of major concerns too? And now that we have moved into the so-called Fourth Age of longer life (*generally now accepted as 80+ years, but this is a dynamic, moving age range*) those concerns are mounting.

It doesn't have to be like that. So I want to try to do something about it. I want to tell you about the people that have inspired me, the 'light bulb' moments that have proved life-changing and the expert opinions from around the world that have illuminated my path forward and helped me put together my personal strategy for preparing for *my* Bigger Future. Everything that I have applied in my own life, you can do, too. I just ask two things of you:

1) INVEST IN YOURSELF
2) BELIEVE IN YOURSELF

If you can do that, if you follow the pathway described in this book, then you will be well on the way to creating your meaningful, happy self, healthy in mind, body and finances and well prepared for Your Bigger Future™, however long it may last.

But let's not get ahead of ourselves! What does this book have in store for you?

My hope is that the content will have universal appeal as I believe that my principles of self-investment and self-belief hold true for everyone. I accept that some parts may be more relevant – or important – to you – than others, depending on your stage in life – whether you are in your 20's, 30's, 40's, 50's, 60's, 70's or later. Here then is a summary, a 'quick start guide' if you like, of the key concepts of the book.

2 YOUR LIFE PATH

Every journey starts with a single step. The first step towards Your Bigger Future™ is recognising your role in life and determining how that knowledge will help you in moving forward – a longevity strategy, if you like.

Embrace the fact that you will get older, but never forget the life events and challenges that have made you who you are today - and who you want to be tomorrow. Nothing beats experience.

Recognise the wow-factor moments that come out of the blue and use those influences to shape your actions and habits. Remain inquisitive.

You're never too old to learn something new. And focus on the future. Focus on staying fit, both physically and mentally. Put your finances in order so that your money will last your lifetime. Seek advice if necessary. Cultivate positive relationships. And always ensure you have a powerful reason for getting up in the morning.

3 HEALTHY BODY

A prerequisite to living a long life is maintaining a healthy constitution. That's a given, surely? It's not just about what we eat, but how and when we eat.

In this chapter, I'll tell you about the healthy eating system that has made a huge, positive difference to my life and to the lives of thousands of others. A Calorie Controlled Lifestyle that is not only about weight loss, but one that actually contributes to body repair and regeneration. It's fun, not famine!

I also examine the scientific propositions that support the notion of extended life beyond anything we could have previously imagined – and the evidence to back it up. I explain why it's not about extending life at all costs, but about quality, long life delivered as a side effect of better health therapies and health maintenance.

4 HEALTHY MIND

A positive mental attitude and clarity of thought will allow you to achieve pretty much everything you want in life for yourself and your family. I'll show you how to keep your mind mentally and physically alert, how to set achievable goals that constantly keep you refreshed and motivated and how to remain focused, committed and confident.

Learn how to reduce stress and anxiety - two of the biggest stumbling blocks to a positive outlook. Develop new habits and routines that will contribute to your optimistic direction in life. You'll come to believe that a decline in cognitive ability as you get older is not necessarily inevitable.

Many age-related transitions which affect the mind are lifestyle-based and can therefore be reduced or eradicated by a re-think and subtle changes to the way you go about your daily life. Sleep, diet and alcohol intake are all major factors to consider. Mental and physical exercises help stimulate the brain and keep it healthy and alert. Read my Top 10 Tips for a healthy mind.

5 HEALTHY PERSONAL FINANCES

Now, with considerably extended lifespans a distinct probability, having enough money to last a lifetime seems to be a universal concern, irrespective of whether a person is wealthy or of modest means.

As a financial consultant, I believe conventional financial planning is an outdated model. Today, financial planning needs to be easy to understand, adaptable and visionary. We need to think much further ahead - not just in terms of years, but decades. And I'm not just talking about pensions. Retirement planning should be directed at securing a regular income, irrespective of its source, to maintain your chosen lifestyle for as long as you live. How do you do that? I'll tell you.

In this chapter, I'll seek to guide you through the basic rules of laying a solid foundation for a lifetime financial strategy. I'll tell you how to estimate and manage the level of income you'll need in retirement, how to build and maintain your capital resource - and the importance of seeking advice if you need it.

You'll learn the basics about popular investment vehicles and the importance of tax-efficiency and estate planning.

In short, I'll pass on to you valuable financial knowledge that I have acquired during the whole of my working life.

6 HEALTHY BUSINESS FINANCES

As the title suggests, you will find this chapter invaluable if you run, or help run, a business, or intend to start an enterprise.

As a relatively successful business partner myself, I have learned a thing or two about building a profitable company. And in the context of this book, improving your financial bottom line to provide for Your Bigger Future™ is what it's all about. If you already operate a profitable company, that's great. But I hope some of the tips and knowledge I have gained over the years could make your business stronger. If you run a young or start-up company, they'll help you to hit the ground running.

I'll tell you about the 14 key areas that should be addressed to ensure success and profitability in virtually any company. I call them 'The Principles for Success in Business.'

I'll also explain why I believe that, although a healthy balance sheet is vital of course, part of the buzz of running any business should be the sheer exhilaration, fun and satisfaction that it brings to you on a personal level.

7 HEALTHY RELATIONSHIPS

Can you imagine how miserable we'd be in our later years if we were lonely? Not a pleasant thought. And yet there are millions of older people worldwide in exactly that position. That's why we all need interactive, enduring relationships with others to lead a happy and fulfilling life.

What does 'being happy' actually mean? What type of relationships can you develop?

Relationships can take many forms of course - from the relationships you have with yourself, your spouse or partner, family and friends and work colleagues, to your leisure time, your pets and the world at large.

In this chapter I cover each category in detail with the ultimate aim of helping you cultivate more meaningful relationships, understanding the needs of others and establishing your personal inner peace and happiness.

I also show you the evidence which proves that people with lots of close, happy relationships have better odds of living a longer life than those who are lonely.

8 SENSE OF PURPOSE

A sense of purpose is a fundamental component of a fulfilling life. Without it, we are prone to boredom, anxiety, depression and often, addictions.

I believe a strong sense of purpose can exert a powerful, positive effect, making us less self-centred and less focused on our own problems.

But what is a 'sense of purpose?' How does it manifest itself? How can we discover our own unique sense of purpose? In this chapter, I'll help you find the answers to those questions, but in essence, a sense of purpose is all about instilling in yourself the knowledge that you are wanted and valued - throughout your life. It's the certainty that we can still be of use, that we can still help others and make a difference, even in our later years.

As a good friend of mine once said, "Life. It's about leaving it better than you found it." That's why a sense of purpose is so important for all of us, for all of our lives.

📖 9 FUN ALONG THE WAY

What's the purpose of life if you can't enjoy it? Sound logic, but we all experience the feeling from time to time that life can sometimes be boring and routine.

It's because we are creatures of habit. Routines are safe, comfortable – and it's human nature to shy away from anything that will take us out of our comfort zone. And there's the rub!

I equate fun with happiness. I believe that having fun, having a laugh and forgetting our concerns, whenever possible, can obviously make us happy, but can also reduce stress, enhance creativity, rebuild energy levels and improve relationships.

Having fun is beneficial for us. I'll show you the research to prove it. And I'll tell you about how my own life experiences showed me that having fun can make you feel... good!

It's not complicated. Even little snippets of fun can make all the difference. Whatever works for you.

So, why not make time for a little more fun in your life. Follow my basic tips in this chapter which will show you how to establish your short and long term 'fun goals.'

If during the course of reading this book you have any questions, comments or observations, please contact me via the companion website www.yourbiggerfuture.co.uk . Here you will find further information, news and a Frequently Asked Questions (FAQ) page.

2 YOUR LIFE PATH

2 YOUR LIFE PATH

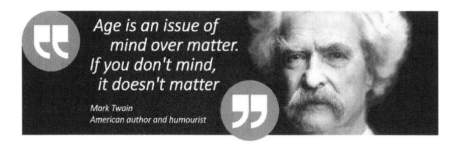

Age is an issue of mind over matter. If you don't mind, it doesn't matter

Mark Twain
American author and humourist

It is important to determine as early as possible what you want to do with your life. What are your personal skills? What do you enjoy doing? What are you good at? What could you become great at to enable you to fulfil your potential? And how might this translate into making a living?

We all recognise single-minded characters that have an unshakeable belief in what they do and nothing will deflect them from their chosen paths in life. But what is it that separates these admired individuals from everyone else? I believe it is because they possessed the wisdom and vision from an early age to be able to foresee and determine their life paths. They believed in themselves and recognised their own personal skills.

We are all, to a greater or lesser extent, the product of our upbringing and environment and are born with certain traits and abilities hard wired into our psyche. Some refer to it as 'factory-installed equipment.' It is the 'optional extras' that really determine what we'll make of our lives, such as identifying and developing our personal skills, work ethic and, to be fair, an element of good luck!

Since my first day at school I've always found communicating with others easy and enjoyable. Later in life I realised I was actually quite good at it. People responded to me positively and I found I was able to influence them in making important and often life-changing decisions for their benefit.

19

I believe that's key to making me a good financial consultant. I am able to listen and evaluate and then communicate and deliver what are very often complicated solutions to my clients that not only improve their positions but also help them develop to their full potential.

When I realised communication was a personal skill, I knew it was something I would always wish to do.

Recognising your role in life - that you actually have a role in life - is I believe the single most important element in creating your longevity strategy. It is the gel that binds everything else together. Later in this book *(Chapter 8, Sense of Purpose)*, I will suggest ways in which you can discover your *raison d'être*.

All too often we hear older people say they no longer have a purpose in life, that they dread getting older. Sadly, my own mother fell into this category in her later years and there was little my brother or I could do to persuade her otherwise. Previously she had been a business woman, maintained a happy family and for many years cared for my father who suffered ill health. When she retired, my brother and I had grown up, my father passed away and her purpose in life evaporated very quickly. As she saw it, there was nothing to replace it.

But it's not just older people that lose their sense of purpose. Other life changing events can have a negative effect on people of all ages. Retirement, the end of a relationship, children leaving home, the death of parents or friends – any of these experiences can impact and damage even the strongest sense of purpose.

Lack of motivation and self-deprecation is negative and will create barriers beyond which you cannot see the way ahead to Your Bigger Future™. For example, embrace the fact that you will get older. It should be a time when you have more confidence (not less), borne out of a lifetime's experience, more wisdom and self-assurance and a time when you will, as my wife says, 'feel more comfortable in your own skin.'

These are forces that you can foresee and influence. But sometimes, every now and then, a significant revelation, a wow-factor moment, comes straight out of the blue and you know immediately it will impact your life forever. This has happened to me three times in recent years.

1. I guess the first revelation was the assertion by leading scientist Aubrey de Grey that **the first person who will live to see their 150th birthday is already in his / her 50s.** Think about that for a moment. Could it be you, or someone that you know?

2. Then I happened to watch a *Horizon* TV documentary presented by Dr. Michael Mosley which proposed *a reduced calorie lifestyle that could regenerate and repair the body in just 12 months.* You may have heard of it. It is called the 5:2 Diet and has thousands of devotees. It proposes a lifestyle that can help us live healthier – for longer. For me, this was not just another 'faddy' diet. It was not all about losing weight. This was a watershed, a life-enhancing system that could allow me to take charge of what was happening to my own body.

3. The third revelation had been staring me in the face for years. And then suddenly I experienced a 'light bulb moment.' Nearly all my financial clients were asking me virtually the same questions, though often couched in different terms.

Will I have enough money? Will my money run out when I get older?

It occurred to me that if my clients harboured those concerns, it was probably a worry shared by many others. A worry that could only be addressed by better financial education and more effective, forward financial planning.

So we're likely to live a lot longer, thanks to advances in medical science, better diets, clean drinking water and (generally) healthier lifestyles. Hopefully we'll be able to fund ourselves for the whole of our lives and we'll have a real sense of purpose.

Job done? Not quite. There is another fundamental requisite to setting your life path. An inquisitive mind. By that I mean we should always strive to continue learning, whatever our age. The great American industrialist Henry Ford said, "Anyone who stops learning is old, whether at 20 or 80. Anyone who keeps learning stays young. The greatest thing in life is to keep your mind young."

I have always been interested in increasing my knowledge, especially on a professional level. For many years, decades even, I have attended business coaching seminars, some in the UK, some in the USA and Canada. Way back in 1999, in Toronto, I participated in an exercise, together with about 40 other like-minded individuals - men and women from all over the world intent on developing their entrepreneurial skills – that made us all re-evaluate our lifespans. The coach asked us to write down a number – the age at which we thought we were going to die! A sobering exercise, to say the least.

It just so happened that I had been reading an article in a British Medical Association journal during the plane journey to Canada which stated that a baby born today (remember this was 1999) could expect to live to 100. I decided to write down the number 90.

The coach then asked us to jot down what position we'd like to be in during *the year before we die*, in respect of the following key areas of our lives:

Physical health
Mental health
Finances
Relationships
Sense of purpose

My response was something along the following lines:
Physical health: At 89, I'd still like to be walking, playing golf and generally keeping fit – and hopefully still enjoying the physical aspects of marriage!
Mental health: I'd hope still to be alert and a good conversationalist.

Finances: Well, I'm a financial consultant. If I can't get that right then it's a poor show! I'd wish to have no money worries with enough income to cover my needs and to be able to help out my family when necessary.

Relationships: Interaction with others is crucial at any age, but more so as we get older. I'd still like to have my loving family around me and regularly meet with good friends.

Sense of purpose: Ideally, even at 89, I'd still like to be engaged in some form of work activity and charitable deeds.

I cover all these areas, and more, later in this book. At the time (1999) they were thought-provoking and revelatory. Today, now that we can expect to live that much longer, it is more relevant than ever that we address those issues.

The next question I think took us by surprise. The coach asked, "If all those areas in your life are good, then how much longer do you think you could live?"

I decided on another 10 years!

At the beginning of the session, the man next to me, Tom, had written down '47' as the age at which he expected to die. He was a Manhattan lawyer - a tough profession to be sure - but that didn't explain his pessimism. The coach tackled him about it.

"Tom, why did you write down '47?"

Tom replied that his father had died from a heart attack aged 47, as had his uncle! So he believed, and always had, that he too would die at 47.

"So what age are you at this present time, Tom?"

"45."

"Tom, this is a three year course. Why did you enrol on a three year course?"

Amusing, of course, but I, together with a few others in the room, persuaded Tom to undergo a full medical, something he'd always avoided. Everything was clear - no health issues whatsoever. It gave him a new impetus and a desire to enjoy life again, to take his time and smell the roses along the way.

The exercise had a very positive effect on me and still does to this day. Now that I'm confident I have much longer to live than I previously imagined, I find that time seems to have slowed down a little. I genuinely feel I have more time to do things.

So, maybe it's time for you to reassess, plan and visualise your own life path?

Bear in mind that:
- You will probably live longer than previous generations
- You have the opportunity to repair and regenerate your body
- If you plan your finances carefully, you should not run out of money
- You'll need to maintain an inquisitive, enquiring mind
- You should define and cultivate your sense of purpose

In this book I have tried to cover all bases so that hopefully you'll discover something of value that will inspire or help you to move forward or improve your life.

Focus on those areas of your life that you know need to be addressed and you will be well on the way to Your Bigger Future™.

Enjoy the journey. I'm sure you will.

TAILPIECE: INSPIRATION

British adventurer Bear Grylls had to overcome a potentially paralysing back injury when, in 1996, during a free-fall parachuting jump in Zambia, his canopy ripped at 16,000 ft, partially opening, causing him to fall and land on his parachute pack on his back, which partially crushed three vertebrae.

According to his surgeon, he came "within a whisker" of being paralyzed for life and at first it was touch and go whether he would ever walk again. He spent the next 12 months in and out of military rehabilitation.

But in a showcase of what pure determination and hard work can do, on 16 May 1998, just 18 months after his accident, he achieved his childhood dream and became one of the youngest people ever to reach the summit of Mount Everest.

Since then he has undertaken many record-breaking exploits that are the stuff of legend and is now well known for his 'outward bound' TV series which regularly feature hair-raising stunts and wilderness survival.

The truth is, I need 10 lifetimes to scratch the surface of the things I'd love to do.

Edward Michael 'Bear' Grylls

3 HEALTHY BODY

3 HEALTHY BODY

*If you want to live
a long life,
shorten your meals*

Benjamin Franklin
American author, politician and
statesman

Have you ever realised how fragile an idea can be? When it comes, if you don't recognise it or are otherwise preoccupied, if you don't grasp it and act on it immediately, it can be lost forever. Brian Wilson of The Beach Boys said, "A genius thought only comes knocking now and then. Just hope to God you are paying attention when it does."

I well remember Lord Robert Winston, the eminent professor of science and society, presenting the analogy of a butterfly flying against the backdrop of a busy New York street with noisy, gridlocked traffic, seemingly thousands of people going about their busy lives amongst huge, concrete skyscrapers. It was almost impossible to spot the butterfly against the frenetic activity in the background. However, when placed against the tranquil pampas plains of Texas, the butterfly was clear to see in all its glory.

If our minds are muddled or unreceptive, or we are busy concentrating on our daily routines, rushing ahead to the next task, new ideas have nowhere to flourish. You have to train your brain to devote time, energy and perseverance to ideas to make them work.

Believe me, I know. In my line of business, financial services, new ideas are what differentiates a successful company from a mediocre one in the marketplace. During my career I very soon came to realise that it was imperative to act on an idea straightaway. It really is a case of 'if you snooze, you lose.' It doesn't necessarily have to be your own original idea – it's the extra 10% you add to it that makes the difference.

So I'm thankful I was 'present' and in a relaxed, receptive frame of mind when I watched a TV Horizon programme presented by Michael Mosley entitled 'Eat, Fast and Live Longer,' because I knew my life would be different from then on. The programme is available to watch on the companion website www.yourbiggerfuture.co.uk .

The facts and ideas put forward by Dr. Mosley, which were genuinely revelationary, were based on scientific studies examining the relationship between what we eat and how long we live and allowed me to see my future life with a clarity and in a way I had never before experienced. It was showing me a life that could potentially be very long – and very healthy! This wasn't about another new, faddish, slimming diet. This was a system that could actually, seriously, prolong life. Let me put it like this. If a world expert said to you – and I quote – "Do this for 12 months and you'll cure yourself," wouldn't you sit up and take note? I certainly did!

Dr. Mosley initially introduced us to Fauja Singh – at 101 the world's oldest marathon runner. Asked for his secret of long life, Fauja said, through an interpreter, that it all came down to a regime that was based on fresh food, small, child-like portions – and regular fasting. He'd had no surgery, had no signs of heart disease and took no medication. This would be pretty remarkable for many 50 year olds, let alone a 101 year old man.

There was the proposition, there and then. It's not just how much or what we eat, but how and when, we eat.

So was this programme actually telling me that if I alternated between eating sensibly and fasting, my body would self-repair and regenerate itself? That I could cure myself, or substantially reduce the risk of some cancers, diabetes, stroke, heart attack and dementia? That I could live a longer, healthier life? The answer was a resounding 'Yes!' (Fasting in this sense does not mean not eating at all. It means that on your 'fast days' you restrict your calorie intake by two-thirds.)

Scientific research has now positively linked calorie restriction to longevity. It's called Calorie Restriction on Optimum Nutrition – CRON.

There are estimated to be about 100,000 people word wide ('Cronies') following this regime of a diet rich in nutrients but low in calories. People who could potentially live longer than those following a normal, 'western diet.' Michael Mosely interviewed Jo, an American man in his 50's who had followed the CRON regime for over 10 years. When subjected to a number of tests, Jo was found to have the constitution of a super athlete. His body fat was just 11.5%.

Dr. Mosley discussed the matter with Professor Luigi Fontana of Washington University. Abdominal fat (visceral fat) is responsible for 40% of deaths in the US and UK. Having too much fat around our waists is seemingly the cause of many of our troubles. As Luigi put it, abdominal fat is the 'bad guy.' The higher the levels of abdominal (visceral) fat, the higher the chance of developing Type 2 Diabetes and cardiovascular diseases – and it can also raise the risk of certain cancers! Professor Fontana proposed that it was virtually impossible for Jo to develop heart problems, simply because he had taken away the symptoms that cause it. He said if Michael adopted this lifestyle he would be 'cured in a year.'

Michael also presented evidence suggesting that calorie restriction can lower the levels of IGF-1 (Insulin-like Growth Factor), one of the drivers partially responsible for ageing. Our bodies go into a completely different mode when we restrict calorie intake. It slows the production of new cells and starts repairing existing ones. DNA damage is likely to be 'fixed' and the development of age-related diseases is slowed right down.

OK, we've known forever that an unhealthy diet full of sugar and saturated fats can undermine health – wherever you may live. In the poorer, under-developed countries, many people die of starvation. In rich countries, many die of over-eating.

It seems to me the choice is simple. Either adopt a calorie-controlled regime, with regular fasting, or, as Dr. Mosley mentioned in the programme, look forward to becoming a typical, 65 year old Westerner relying on a daily average of 6 – 8 drugs to get through each day!

Michael Mosley believes this system could radically change our lives for the better. His view is that it is not so much about wanting to live 'forever,' but living longer – healthier. His recommendation is rather less daunting. Intermittent fasting – two days of reduced calories per week, with the other five days of eating 'normal' food. It's called, rather unsurprisingly, the 5:2 diet (which can be reduced to a '6:1 diet' when your target weight is achieved), but I prefer to refer to it as a Calorie-Controlled Lifestyle (CCL), because I don't like the word 'diet.' To me, 'diet' sounds like hard work, a temporary 'fix' which is ineffective long-term. Living a healthy lifestyle should be fun, realistic, positive and sustainable.

So do I practice what I preach? I certainly do! In the first three weeks following the CCL regime, I lost nearly 14 lbs in weight. Within several months I'd lost approximately 28lbs.

A number of friends that I have recommended to the CCL system have not initially understood the concept of 'calorie control' and have been disappointed with their modest weight loss. They mistakenly thought that if they restricted their calorie intake on two days a week, they could literally eat anything on the other five days. Not so! You still have to keep a close eye on your calorie intake every day, not just on your 'reduced calorie' days, to ensure you do not exceed your official, daily recommended amount too often.

But of course the CCL is not all about weight loss and looks. For me, it's about keeping healthy, body repair and regeneration.

And here is another surprising and possibly related benefit. Three years ago I purchased a very nice, but very expensive pair of Gucci-framed glasses as my eyesight was beginning to deteriorate.

I now don't need them! I discussed this with an optician friend who said that whilst eyesight can sometimes improve as we age, he was nevertheless surprised by my observations!

So, could this be as a result of my body regenerating itself? I can't think of any other explanation. My wife certainly didn't agree with me 'paying a fortune' for the glasses anyway and is even more scathing now that they don't even come out of their case!

Attaining your optimum weight should be a goal for us all and the NHS Height to Weight ratio chart reproduced here gives the official, recommended guidelines.

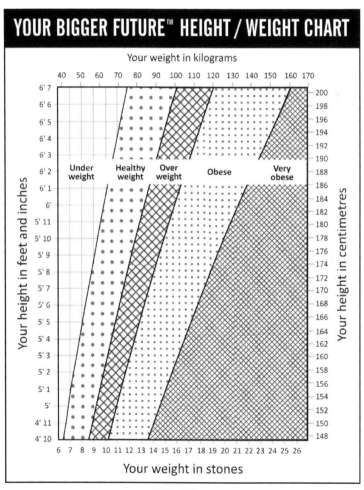

NHS guidelines.
This chart is only suitable for adult men and women. It isn't suitable for children or young people under 18.

33

If you are in the underweight range there could be a number of reasons for this and your GP should be your first port of call for advice. If you are in the healthy weight range – congratulations, but don't rest on your laurels. To stay in good health you'll need to continue to eat sensibly and of course I would heartily recommend the Calorie Controlled Lifestyle system that has worked for me. And don't forget to maintain your exercise, or activity, routine. According to Government guidelines, moderate exercise recommendation is about 30 minutes a day, or 150 minutes a week. A brisk walk is fine.

If you find yourself in any of the other weight ranges then, unless you are for example, a professional rugby player with well-developed musculature, clearly you are heavier than you should be and are at increased risk of heart disease, stroke and Type 2 Diabetes.

It may be useful at this stage to take a moment and explore just what a calorie is and how you can monitor your intake.

A calorie is a unit of energy. It can refer to energy *consumption* through eating and drinking and energy *usage* through physical activity. For example, an apple may contain 80 calories, whilst a one mile walk may use up about 100 calories, dependent on your height and weight.

Your body is a machine that needs an optimum amount of calories to run itself. On average, a man needs 2000 calories a day, depending on age, height and activity and a woman requires about 1500 – to 'run' our bodies. And that's just if we lie in bed all day and do nothing! Calorie intake needs to increase to about 2400 for a man and 1800 for a woman to fuel the daily routines of life – going to work, walking, talking, eating and taking moderate exercise. Generally, anything more than this puts weight on and anything less, or more rigorous exercise, reduces weight.

Essentially these numbers are general guidelines. To calculate your recommended calorie intake, I recommend you visit www.calculator.net/calorie where you will be able to input your personal data and get your personal numbers. Knowing your numbers is the start of everything!

Keeping track of your calorie intake can be difficult and it's easy to lose your way. I use the MyFitnessPal app calorie counter which allows you to enter a target weight (https://www.myfitnesspal.com/). *(It's free!)* I have found it incredibly useful as it also makes me accountable to myself. *(Other calorie-counting apps are available!)*

For me, the 5:2, CCL approach has manifestly benefitted me in many ways. In addition to weight loss, I have also reduced my alcohol intake. Alcohol was never a major issue for me, but I realised my consumption was gradually creeping up. Previously I had tried 'no drinking days,' without much success, but having to count calories meant I just had to cut out alcohol on my 'fast' days in order to maintain my required daily quota.

My sleep pattern has improved. I now awake feeling fresher and brighter and more ready for the day ahead.

In essence, the beauty of the CCL is that I can still eat 'normally,' just not so much! When my stomach rumbles on a 'fast' day, instead of thinking about eating I remember that my body is regenerating itself and that I can look forward to the next day when I'm free to eat what I want – within reason! But I rarely, if ever, indulge in a food binge, and this is borne out by the experience of others on calorie controlled lifestyles. You may find, like me, that you really don't want to eat quite so much, anyway.

And what about the types of food we should be consuming? Well I'm not about to lecture you on what you should and shouldn't eat. There is a mass of information available – online, in print, on TV and anecdotal – for you to make up your own mind. Whether we consider ourselves food experts or not, and whether we admit it to ourselves, we all know which particular foods are good for us and which aren't. I would however recommend you visit the 5:2 fast diet™ web site www.thefastdiet.co.uk where you'll find lots of useful advice.

Personally, I know I can eat and drink pretty much what I want – but within reason, as I said. I eat lots of fresh fruit and vegetables every day, some fish or meat, oats, nuts, seeds, yoghurts – and the occasional dessert! You may find it difficult to stick to the CCL initially, but the rewards can be huge. The secret is smaller, more controlled portions. (Remember Fauja Singh? Fresh food, small portions and regular fasting.)

It's all about making sensible choices in the food we eat – and very importantly – the quantity we consume. Find out what works for you and decide on your goal. Aim to remain as fit and healthy as possible for as long as possible so that, for example, you can spend more quality time with your family and friends, or continue to participate in your favourite sport.

And talking of sport, what about exercise? No-one can argue against the fact that exercise plays a crucial role in maintaining a strong, healthy body. OK, we can't all be super athletes but we should all endeavour to look after our bodies in the best way possible. Walking, jogging, golf, tennis, swimming, cycling and visiting the gym are all excellent ways to enjoy keeping fit. Just make sure you do something on a regular basis that makes you perspire, something that raises your heart rate and 'stretches' you. Choose an activity that you can realistically fit into your day. I run two or three times a week, play golf regularly and feel regenerated and invigorated each time.

A calorie counting app, in conjunction with an exercise recorder can log your exercise and produce a 'net' calorie count for the day. I use the STRAVA app which links to My Fitness Pal, both of which are free. *(Other apps are available!)* It's a bit like a spy in the camp. Once set up you can't cheat it!

For me, recording how much I eat, drink and exercise each day has become a habit – the norm. Remember the old adage 'A moment on the lips is a lifetime on the hips?' A yummy chocolate digestive biscuit contains about 100 calories, but to burn those calories you'll need to take a brisk, 15 minute walk or run a mile!

You need to know all your numbers! You need to know what weight you'd like to be and you should monitor your visceral fat and body mass index, body fat, blood pressure, and cholesterol. Many pharmacists provide free blood pressure and cholesterol tests.

DIY devices for monitoring these functions and conditions at home are universally available from many high street retail outlets and online at very reasonable cost. I have purchased and found these devices very useful, in particular:

- OMRON BF508 Body Composition and Body Fat Monitor, which measures weight, visceral fat classification, body fat percentage and BMI calculation. Cost around £50.
- OMRON Automatic Blood Pressure Monitor. Cost from £20 upwards, depending on sophistication.

(Other brands are available!)

It's important to be consistent when you take your readings. I take mine after my reduced calorie days.

Here are the guidelines recommended by various respected institutions.

HEALTHY BODY NUMBERS / BODY MASS INDEX

CLASSIFICATION	BMI SCORE (kg/m2)
Underweight	< 18.5
Normal	18.5 - 24.9
Overweight	25.0 - 29.0
Obese	30.0 - 40.0
Extremely obese	> 40.0

National Heart, Lung and Blood Institute guidelines

HEALTHY BODY NUMBERS / BODY FAT
Healthy v. unhealthy levels of fatness for males and females of different ages

GENDER	FATNESS	BF%: AGE 20-39	BF%: AGE 40-59	BF%: AGE 60-79
MALE	Underfat	< 8%	< 11%	< 13%
	Normal	8 - 20%	11 - 22%	13 - 25%
	Overfat	20 - 25%	22 - 28%	25 - 30%
	Obese	> 25%	> 28%	> 30%
FEMALE	Underfat	< 21%	< 23%	< 24%
	Normal	21 - 33%	23 - 34%	24 - 36%
	Overfat	33 - 39%	34 - 40%	36 - 42%
	Obese	> 39%	> 40%	> 42%

Based on World Health Organisation guidelines

HEALTHY BODY NUMBERS / ABDOMINAL / VISCERAL FAT

VISCERAL FAT LEVEL	LEVEL CLASSIFICATION
1 - 9	0 (Normal)
10 - 14	+ (High)
15 - 30	+ + (Very High)

Omron Healthcare

HEALTHY BODY NUMBERS / BLOOD PRESSURE

CATEGORY	SYSTOLIC BLOOD PRESSURE (mmHG)	DIASTOLIC BLOOD PRESSURE (mmHG)
NORMAL	< 120	< 80
PRE-HYPERTENSION	120 - 139	80 - 89
STAGE 1 HYPERTENSION	140 - 159	90 - 99
STAGE 2 HYPERTENSION	≥ 160	≥ 100

Pre-hypertension is a warning sign that you may develop high blood pressure in the future.
Stage 1 hypertension is the beginning stage of high blood pressure.
Stage 2 hypertension is severe high blood pressure.

Based on Joint National Committee on Prevention, Detection, Evaluation and Treatment of High Blood Pressure guidelines

Explanatory Note: Blood pressure is the force of the blood pushing against the walls of your arteries. Blood pressure is usually described as your systolic blood pressure over your diastolic blood pressure, e.g. 120/80. This is measured in millimetres of mercury (mmHg). Systolic blood pressure refers to the pressure in the arteries when the heart beats. Diastolic blood pressure is the pressure in the arteries between heart beats. An optimal blood pressure reading is 120/80 mmHg or less. High blood pressure (higher than 140/90 mmHg), known as hypertension, can weaken blood vessels and damage organs. Left untreated, high blood pressure can lead to conditions such as stroke, heart failure or kidney failure. (Source: Omron Healthcare)

HEALTHY BODY NUMBERS / CHOLESTEROL

	UNIT	OPTIMAL	INTERMEDIATE	HIGH
Total Cholesterol	mmol/L	< 5.2	5.3 - 6.2	> 6.2
LDL Cholesterol	mmol/L	< 3.36	3.36 - 4.11	> 4.11
HDL Cholesterol	mmol/L	> 1.55	1.03 - 1.55	< 1.03

Note: Cholesterol is carried in the blood attached to proteins called lipoproteins. There are two main forms, LDL (low density lipoprotein) and HDL (high density lipoprotein). LDL cholesterol is often referred to as "bad cholesterol" because too much is unhealthy. HDL is often referred to as "good cholesterol" because it is protective.
mmol/L = millimoles per litre. Source: NHS guidelines.

I should point out that these charts are for information and general guidance only. I'm not a doctor and I'm not qualified to dispense medical advice, but the charts have been produced by experts. If you are concerned about your health, or have any underlying health problems, please consult your GP or other qualified medical professional.

I find a great way to keep a check on my numbers and set targets is with a chart of my own (what else?). This was my original chart:

YOUR BIGGER FUTURE™ HEALTHY BODY NUMBERS

Start date: 31/8/14	STARTING NUMBERS	TARGET NUMBERS	TARGET DATE	MONTH 1	MONTH 3	MONTH 6
Weight	191 lbs ----------- 86.7 kilos	161 lbs ----------- 73 kilos	August 2015	180 lbs ----------- 81 kilos	175 lbs ----------- 79 kilos	167 lbs ----------- 75.8 kilos
Body mass index (BMI)	30%	23%	August 2015	29%	25%	24.6%
Body fat	29%	20%	August 2015	29%	26%	22.6%
Abdominal / Visceral fat	12%	7%	August 2015	11%	10%	9%
Blood pressure	Systolic- 135 Diastolic- 86 Pulse- 80	Systolic- 130 Diastolic- 85 Pulse- 70	August 2015	Systolic- 134 Diastolic- 85 Pulse- 75	Systolic- 130 Diastolic- 84 Pulse- 70	Systolic- 128 Diastolic- 83 Pulse- 68
Cholesterol	5.3	' well below 5 mmol/L '	August 2015	5.1	4.9	4.8

You'll find a blank template at the end of this book or download it from www.yourbiggerfuture.co.uk

I believe this chart proves it works. You may find your 'starting' numbers a little alarming, but take stock of where you are, decide where you want to be, lay out you plans and then just do it!

The pressure to eat unhealthily can be overwhelming and regular exercise is a big commitment, but a sensible eating option, combined with your chosen exercise programme will eventually become a healthy habit. You need to call on every ounce of willpower at your disposal to focus on your goal to stay healthier for longer in preparation for Your Bigger Future™.

****

Can we really believe Dr. Aubrey de Grey's prediction that the first person to live to 150 is already in his / her 50s and that the first person to live to 1,000 will soon be born?

An Indonesian man, Mbah Gotho claims he is the world's oldest man *(August 2016, Daily Mail)* at 145 years of age and his date of birth, 31 December 1870, appears to have been verified by official records. So the prediction may not be as far-fetched as some might think.

Let's look at what Dr. de Grey has to say to back up his theory.

He is a British, biomedical gerontologist, chief scientist of the SENS foundation dedicated to longevity research and author of a number of publications on the subject. His work has been supported by some very serious investors, including Peter Thiel, co-founder of PayPal.

Dr. de Grey believes that within his own lifetime, doctors will possess all the tools they need to 'cure' ageing by banishing all disease and extending life expectancy indefinitely. He describes ageing as the life-long accumulation of multiple molecular and cellular damage throughout the body. His vision of the future, the very near future, in fact, is of a time

41

when we'll visit our doctors for regular 'maintenance,' or preventative geriatrics, which will include gene and stem cell therapies and immune stimulation to repair that damage and keep us in good shape. In effect he's talking about getting older without ageing.

Exactly how far and how fast life expectancy will increase is of course subject to debate. But the trend is clear and is supported by demographic fact. An average of three months is added to life expectancy every year and experts believe there will be 1,000,000 centenarians worldwide by the year 2030. (There were 44,000 in 2010.)

However, other experts believe that this trend may falter due to the 'western world' 'epidemic' of obesity which is now also becoming apparent in developing countries.

Perhaps not surprisingly, Aubrey de Grey is not without his detractors. Some have described his theories as 'pseudo-science,' but no-one has been able to counter them with hard scientific data or fact. And for some, the prospect of living for hundreds of years is not particularly attractive, as it conjures up visions of generations of sick, weak people and a society unable to cope. For de Grey it is a case of keeping the killer diseases at bay.

He says, "This is absolutely not a matter of keeping people alive in a bad state of health. This is about preventing people getting sick as a result of old age. The particular therapies that we are working on will only deliver long life as a side-effect of delivering better health."

Dr. de Grey divides the damage caused by ageing into a number of categories for which repair techniques need to be developed if his prediction for continual maintenance is to be realised. For some categories, the science is still in its earliest stages, but there are other areas where it's already almost there. For example, stem cell therapies are currently being trialled in people with spinal cord injuries, and de Grey and others say they may one day be used to find ways to repair disease-damaged brains and hearts.

He is reluctant to make firm predictions about how long people will be able to live in the future, but he does say that with each major advance in longevity, scientists will buy more time to make yet more scientific progress. In his view, this means that the first person who will live to 1,000 is likely to be born within the next 20 years.

He says, "I call it longevity escape velocity - where we have a sufficiently comprehensive panel of therapies to enable us to push back the ill health of old age faster than time is passing.

"There really shouldn't be any limit *(on life expectancy)* imposed by how long ago you were born. The whole point of maintenance is that it works indefinitely."

Aubrey de Grey is not a lone voice crying in the wilderness. His views are supported by other celebrated authorities such as futurist, physicist and author, Dr. Michio Kaku. And I'm reminded of something a good friend once said to me. "If you can't dispute the logic, you must accept the conclusions."

There is also another aspect to consider. Could *working longer* actually be good for us? Well, I've always thought so, but now the UK Government's Chief Medical Officer, Professor Sally Davies officially agrees with me! In her 2016 Annual report called, 'Baby Boomers: Fit for the Future,' she proposes that people of 'retirement age' should try to stay in work (or get involved in community and voluntary activities) *to keep their minds and bodies in better condition.*

Michael Mosley's research and Aubrey de Grey's predictions have had a profound effect on me. They've caused me to stop and reconsider my future. And they've convinced me that we can look forward to a much longer, healthier future – time we previously (subconsciously I suppose) never thought we'd have. I'm thinking of all those extra things we'll be able to do, all those new people we'll be able to meet, the new places we'll be able to visit – and the extra time we'll have with our families and friends.

HEALTHY BODY QUICK START TIPS

1. Be inspired! Watch the BBC Horizon programme, 'Eat, Fast and Live Longer,' available at
www.yourbiggerfuture.co.uk
or
http://www.bbc.co.uk/iplayer/episode/b01lxyzc/horizon-20122013-3-eat-fast-and-live-longer

2. Know your numbers. Invest in monitors and use the ready-made template *Your Bigger Future™ Healthy Body Numbers* (available at the end of this book) to design your Calorie Controlled Lifestyle strategy.

3. Be clear on the amount of calories you need to consume each day. Find out at www.calculator.net/calorie . Download a calorie-counting app, e.g. MyFitnessPal, to record your food intake and an app such as STRAVA to record your exercise routine.

4. Always be conscious that you are what you eat and drink. Ask yourself, 'Is this food doing me any good, or does it just taste nice?'

5. On the basis that you want to reduce your weight, or maintain your optimum weight, start with two reduced calorie days a week until you achieve your target weight, then maintain one reduced calorie day a week – forever! But don't forget - the Calorie Controlled Lifestyle is not just about losing weight - it's also about maintaining a healthy, regenerative body!

TAILPIECE: INSPIRATION

A little while ago I watched the great Gary Player – one of the world's greatest golfers and author of many memorable quotations – being interviewed during The Open in Scotland.

At 80 years young, he is in amazing shape, perhaps not surprisingly for a man that starts every day with 1,300 sit-ups and pushing 300lb on a leg machine! When at home in South Africa, he rises every day at 5am and spends 12 hours working on his farm.

He said, "Retirement is a death warrant. I'm 80 and I'm still the same as when I was 22. I'm still curious to learn, and I don't believe in retirement. I want to die working. I feel very blessed to reach such an age in such condition but it's also my reward for looking after myself all these years. It frustrates me when I look around and see so many young people eating too much and getting fat. Why is more not being done to teach them you can't do anything without your health?"

As for me, I'll never stop. When I'm 90 I'll still play golf.

Gary Player

THOUGHT FOR THE DAY: HEALTHY BODY

What have I done, or will I do, to improve or maintain my health - yesterday / today / tomorrow?

4 HEALTHY MIND

4 HEALTHY MIND

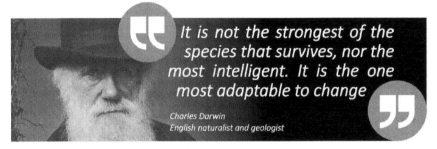

It is not the strongest of the species that survives, nor the most intelligent. It is the one most adaptable to change

Charles Darwin
English naturalist and geologist

A mentally healthy mind

A positive mental attitude is clearly the key to achieving pretty much everything you want in life for yourself and your family. Clarity of thought is what will allow you to see the big picture – Your Bigger Future™.

So how do we keep our minds mentally and physically alert and healthy? How do we define a healthy mind? I believe the first step is having a clear, but flexible, vision of your life ahead. The winds of life keep changing and you need to constantly trim your sails to make sure you are always heading in the right direction.

Dan Sullivan, CEO of Strategic Coach® has been a huge inspiration to me for many years and (with his permission) I intend to refer to his wisdom and vision in this chapter.

He once posed a question to me that provided the bedrock for my personal big picture thinking – the Dan Sullivan Question® – "If we were meeting here again in three years' time, what has to have happened both personally and professionally for you to feel happy with your progress?"

It was a great question. Insightful and thought-provoking. But why, I asked, just three years? He explained that three years is tangible. It's the year after the year after next. Five or ten years in the future would be too distant for most people to realistically envisage.

I realised this concept could form the basis for a system of setting achievable goals over successive three year timescales that would constantly keep me refreshed and motivated. This is a snapshot of mine in 2015:

YOUR BIGGER FUTURE™ ACHIEVABLE GOALS

THIS QUARTER'S GOALS	1 YEAR GOALS	3 YEAR GOALS	LIFETIME GOALS
Family and friends			
By December 2015 - to keep close to all family and support as much as possible. Help youngest get a new job.	By December 2016 - to have helped son and daughter settle into life in London, to have helped elder daughter with wedding, to help step son with golfing endeavours and step daughter with career choices.	By December 2018 - to have helped all children secure good jobs and be happy at work and play.	To have been the best inspiring, encouraging husband, dad, step-dad, brother, son and friend I could be.
Work and financial			
To have agreed all targets and budgets for 2016.	To have achieved targets, by making reasonable profit and to have expanded and moved to larger offices and for funds under management to be increased.	For the company to have achieved its 3 year profit forecasts and capital value to have increased.	To have helped drive, direct and develop our company to the best of my ability.
Fitness and health			
Sort my foot operation and get knees checked again.	Run two or three times a week, play regular golf and get handicap down to 10. Eat and drink healthily and keep to Calorie Controlled Lifestyle.	Run two or three times a week, play regular golf and get handicap down to 8. Eat and drink healthily and keep to Calorie Controlled Lifestyle.	To be as fit as possible having followed a Calorie Controlled Lifestyle and be free of preventable diseases.
Wild card things!			
To plan my 5th charity challenge and learn to ski for it!	To have handed over a charity cheque for £12K to the children's oncology playroom at local hospital.	To have our company 2018 charity year planned and coming together.	To have had fun, helped raise money for charities and to have 'pushed myself' and achieved as much as practically possible.

This may work for you, too. I was amazed how focused I became, because I had made a commitment to myself. Give it a go. Make your own list and get started!

(A blank template can be found at the end of this book or downloaded from www.yourbiggerfuture.co.uk)

You'll need one more ingredient to supplement your commitment. Confidence. Confidence that you can realistically pursue your ambitions. I like to think of confidence as the electricity of life. It's a very important component of life. Without it, very little works as efficiently as it could.

This very subject arose when I was on holiday with a group of friends. We were all of a 'certain age.' One said he felt that as he got older, his confidence was beginning to wane. I asked him why he felt that way, when he was at the time of his life when his cumulative life experiences should have given him all the confidence in the world. It transpired he was worried about the frailties of ageing and the health problems that might lie ahead for him. He couldn't see beyond that and picture a positive future.

Of course, lack of confidence – a dimming of the electricity of life, if you like – can affect us all at times. What's needed is a charging system that can boost confidence and a procedure we can follow all the time. I've discovered that actually committing to paper the things that give me confidence and referring to them on a regular basis, has an enormously positive effect on me. This is my 10-point Confidence Booster:

YOUR BIGGER FUTURE™ CONFIDENCE BOOSTER
What gives me confidence?

1	Having sufficient spare money
2	Having good clients and excellent prospects
3	Delegating and getting my work done faster
4	Being 'over target' in business
5	Spending quality time with my wife and family
6	Making home improvements
7	Visualising a big future for the company
8	Keeping fit and healthy and enjoying exercise
9	Having a tidy office and a tidy home
10	Having holiday breaks planned

My wife's is very different — and shorter!

YOUR BIGGER FUTURE™ CONFIDENCE BOOSTER	
What gives me confidence?	
1	Knowing my children and husband are happy, safe and well
2	Having great and trusted friends around me
3	Dressing appropriately
4	Always striving to do the best I can each day
5	Getting enough sleep
6	Keeping as fit and healthy as possible for my family

Try it yourself — and here's a tip. Print it out on card and carry it with you as a regular reminder and confidence-building tool. It works for me.

(A blank template can be found at the end of this book or downloaded from www.yourbiggerfuture.co.uk)

Stress and anxiety can also be major stumbling blocks when it comes to envisaging Your Bigger Future™. Today, in life, as in business, stress comes with the territory, with demands on our time and abilities flying at us from all directions. How often have you found yourself in an uncomfortable situation — you're somewhere you don't want to be or you've been asked to do something you don't want to do?

Some years ago I was privileged to be a member of the local Round Table, a charitable organisation of professionals that get together for friendship with the ultimate aim of helping the community. It was great. We had some wonderful times, engaging in various exciting activities and providing help and support for local people. However, I had a wife and growing family and I began to realise that my Round Table activities — the regular meetings, the organisation of events — were beginning to impinge on my family life. I started to stress out over the fact that my nearest and dearest were having to take a back seat. It just couldn't continue. I realised I was in a 'mess.' Although I felt I had an obligation (to the Round Table), I no longer had the commitment. As I saw it, the only option open to me was to quit the organisation. My family had to come first. As soon as I did that – and it was hard – I experienced a massive sense of relief and my stress and anxiety disappeared.

Stress can affect anyone, at any time. An acquaintance of mine, an entrepreneur and business / life coach from Canada, found himself with a problem. His elderly mother had become difficult, cantankerous and highly demanding of his time. No matter what he did and how much time he spent with her, it wasn't good enough. His own family life began to suffer and his stress levels shot up. And then one day, the truth dawned on him. He was responsible *to* his Mum to the best of his abilities, but he was not responsible *for* her. His anxiety subsided.

I experienced a similar dilemma. My career as a financial consultant can be stressful at times. There were occasions when I used to get very upset when something went wrong (usually beyond my control, such as a fall in the stock markets) and my investment clients became disadvantaged. I felt I had failed in my obligation. But I came to realise that whilst I had no control over the markets, I did control the services I provided for my clients, such as tax-efficient products, a centralised investment system backed by solid research and judgement, together with regular communication to keep them informed and up-to-date. I reasoned that I was responsible *to* my clients, but I could not be responsible *for* them.

Similarly, in a broader sense, we are responsible to the world but not for what happens in it! The truth is, altruism, selflessness, benevolence and commitment to the welfare of others can only go so far. We cannot forever beat ourselves up trying to improve the lives of others to the detriment of our own. Sometimes we just have to discipline ourselves to a different mind-set.

Habits and discipline are fundamental founding principles of a strong direction in life. Dan Sullivan, creator and founder of The Strategic Coach® Program coaches that the only difference between successful people and unsuccessful people is that successful people have successful habits. We are all 100% disciplined to our existing set of habits. You may hear people say that they wish they were more disciplined. What they probably mean, although often they don't realise it, is that they wish they had a better set of habits.

We can change our habits, of course. Did you know that according to behavioural science studies, it takes just 21 days to get rid of a bad habit and establish a new one? Just imagine, within 12 months you could be a brand new you if you wanted to be! I found that jotting down my habits on paper in a chart format and then committing myself to change or improve those habits, was a good starting point. You probably realise by now that I love charts and diagrams. That's because, for me, they help solidify an idea or concept. This was my original, working chart which essentially follows the chapter subjects in this book:

YOUR BIGGER FUTURE™ HABIT ADJUSTER

CATEGORY	MY CURRENT HABITS	HOW I CAN IMPROVE THIS HABIT?
Healthy body	I do regular exercise. I try to eat only healthy food.	Run two or three times a week and continue to eat and drink healthily but *monitor* my consumption in line with a Calory Controlled Lifestyle.
Healthy mind	I know my strengths and direct others to work to theirs.	Delegate the tasks I don't enjoy to those more suited to them - make use of the personal skills of others.
Healthy finances	Working towards developing the company and improving its value.	Study weekly reports of cash flow. Be more assertive in the development of new and beneficial products and services.
Healthy relationships	I spend as much time as possible with family. I try to keep people informed as much as possible and pass on ideas to help others achieve their goals.	Develop and improve our client communication systems. Spend more quality time with family and friends.
Healthy sense of purpose	I visualise the bigger picture and aim others towards it. I follow projects through.	Discuss my vision in more detail with colleagues and share my drive and enthusiasm.
Having fun	I play golf and enjoy motorcycling. I have a large circle of friends and enjoy socialising.	Improve my golf with coaching lessons. Take more time out for non-work-related activities!

Why not try something similar, if you are not doing so already?
(A blank template can be found at the end of this book or downloaded from www.yourbiggerfuture.co.uk)

I have developed a couple of regular habits that may also help you. The first I call my '3-2-1' habit. It works like this. At the end of each day, I think of three things that happened during the day that were good. Then I think of two things that were OK and acceptable. Finally I think of the one thing that happened that was not so good – the thing that I would maybe do differently if given a second chance. It's a simple thought process that can help develop better habits.

My second habit is to complete a regular journal, in which I ask myself a number of set questions that I believe have a great relevance in focusing and exercising my mind. If time allows, I prefer to do this as often as possible, first thing in the morning, but any time in the day is OK – whatever suits you. I date each entry so that I can refer back to it if necessary. The questions follow very closely the thoughts for the day that I have popped in at the end of most of the chapters of this book. This is one of my typical page examples:

YOUR BIGGER FUTURE™ JOURNAL   5th December 2016

PHYSICAL HEALTH
What have I done, or will I do, to improve or maintain my health - yesterday / today / tomorrow?

Yesterday	Reduced calorie day - just 900 net calories!
Today	Normal calorie controlled day (2000 calories). Will walk dogs later.
Tomorrow	Another normal calorie controlled day. Will go for a run.

MENTAL HEALTH
What have I done, or will I do, to boost my confidence - yesterday / today / tomorrow?

Yesterday	Good reduced calorie day / Managed to resolve some work problems.
Today	Interesting work day planned.
Tomorrow	Looking forward to good client meeting / Out with friends in evening.

PERSONAL MONEY
What have I done, or will I do, to make or save money - yesterday / today / tomorrow?

Yesterday	Decided to shop around for better deal on my TV and phone subscriptions.
Today	Working on big client case that will go towards my personal income target.
Tomorrow	Another client appointment - again, potentially good for my personal target.

BUSINESS MONEY
What have I done, or will I do, to improve my business - yesterday / today / tomorrow?

Yesterday	Worked on our new business plan.
Today	See co-directors and chat through my business plan ideas
Tomorrow	Work on financial data.

RELATIONSHIPS
Who and what do I value? Does anything need to change - yesterday / today / tomorrow?

Yesterday	Family / friends / work colleagues / clients.
Today	Clear outstanding client work.
Tomorrow	Make sure I speak to son before his holiday.

SENSE OF PURPOSE
Who did I, or will I, help to have a better day - yesterday / today / tomorrow?

Yesterday	Worked on book (this book!) It will hopefully help many people.
Today	Discussed book with two clients. They were very encouraging and interested.
Tomorrow	Ensure company news ebulletin goes out.

HAVING FUN
What was a fun activity yesterday? What will be fun today / tomorrow?

Yesterday	Enjoyed a good run with my dog.
Today	Hopefully play golf or practice.
Tomorrow	Out tonight with friends.

(A blank template can be found at the end of this book or downloaded from www.yourbiggerfuture.co.uk)

Developing better habits is all about change. We need to know how to adapt, improve and adjust to a constantly changing environment and set of values. Life is complicated. It's a truism, sure enough, but when we realise and accept that, it's surprising how much easier it is to cope with everything that the modern world throws at us. By all means start out with basic aims in mind, but accept that your life will not follow a smooth, straight path and be prepared for diversions along the way. Some of these diversions may be unexpected but will often excite, stimulate and motivate you to greater things. You'll come to accept that maybe your finest hour is yet to come, and that's a great feeling, you know. It keeps you interested and alert to new possibilities.

The ability to adapt to change is a prerequisite for a longer, happier existence. Change is happening all around us, all the time. In economic terms it's referred to as 'creative destruction.' In other words, new ideas, technology and advances come along constantly. The concept was popularised in the 1950s by the Austrian-American economist Joseph Schumpeter. He described 'creative destruction' as "a process of industrial mutation that incessantly revolutionises the economic structure from within, incessantly destroying the old one, incessantly creating a new one." The incredible advances in IT is a perfect example of this in the modern age.

Most of us embrace this change because it improves our lives. Other changes may be more gradual and take us unawares. If we do not have our wits about us we can be blindsided and then it can be too late to adapt. I remember reading Charles Handy's seminal book 'The Age of Unreason' over 20 years ago. It proposed that it is necessary to break out of old ways of thinking in order to use change to our advantage. In the book he gave the example of 'the frog in the jam jar effect.' He claimed that if you put a frog in water and slowly heat it, the frog will eventually allow itself to be boiled to death, so subtle is the rise in temperature. I don't know whether this is a fact or not, but the analogy is clear. We should recognise change and adapt to it.

It's all part of that positive mental attitude to which I referred at the beginning of the chapter. But what does positive mental attitude *actually* mean? Yes, it's about a clear vision of your future, confidence and good habits, but it's also about being 'present.'

How can I illustrate this? Well, how about this. Have you ever been at a party, in conversation with someone, when you suddenly realise that person is just 'not there.' They are preoccupied. Maybe their minds are elsewhere or they are just looking around. OK, it could be they find you boring and uninteresting, but the effect is that it may make you feel belittled and unimportant. Conversely, when someone pays you attention, looks at you and is engaged, you are drawn to that person and tend to want to spend more time with them. That's what I believe being 'present' is all about. It's about being aware of the 'here and now' – the moment you are in – making the best use of your time and not missing an opportunity because your mind was elsewhere. I also believe that those who practice 'Mindfulness' (awareness of and living in the present moment) tend to experience greater health and well-being.

Dan Sullivan of Strategic Coach® says, "Wherever you are, make sure you are there."

■■

A physically healthy mind

Now let's consider the other equally important aspect of maintaining a healthy mind – the physical condition of your brain. It may be interesting to hear what the experts have to say on the subject of cognitive ability (i.e. the mental process of awareness, perception, reasoning and judgement) and its decline throughout our lives.

According to research published in 2015, psychologists Joshua Hartshorne and Laura Germine tested 21,926 people aged 10 to 71 who had visited the website TestMyBrain.org. for their abilities to think quickly and recall information – also known as fluid intelligence. Participants were tested on vocabulary, the ability to encode strings of numbers into symbols, something called the "mind in the eyes" test, an emotion-recognition test which asks people to identify someone's feelings using only a picture of their eyes, and working memory—that is, the ability to recall recently viewed objects.

The study found that different components of fluid intelligence peak at different ages, some as late as age 40. Some of the youngest participants did best on the number-to-symbol coding task, with the peak performance around 19 or 20 years old. After that, performance steadily declined with age. Working memory peaked between the mid-20s to mid-30s before beginning a relatively slow decline.

Those over 40 shouldn't fret, though. On the "mind in the eyes" test, participants abilities peaked at age 48, after which emotion-recognition skills declined very slowly. Vocabulary, meanwhile, climbed with the participants' age, and gave little sign of slowing down.

The point of the study wasn't really to identify what age we peak at or which ability reaches its apex later. Rather, as Hartshorne and Germine reported, the study aimed to show that cognitive abilities don't all peak at the same time or even follow any one trend as people age. Some of the trends are likely due to biological decline, while others, such as the steady increase in vocabulary, could be the result of the experience of age.

There's a lot of encouragement to be gained from that study. To me, it indicates that a steady decline in cognitive ability as we age is not necessarily a done deal.

The subject that many of us find difficult to address is that of Alzheimer's, a form of which, dementia, has probably touched us all by association in some form or another. My own mother, as I mentioned previously, sadly suffered from dementia and it eventually led to her death at the age of 90. The old adage – 'that's a good age' – is true, but how much more fulfilling life would be if we could reach that age – and older – without suffering mental decline.

It's a fact that more people over the age of 55 now fear developing dementia more than cancer. (It's also a fact that the fastest-growing age group in the USA is the over 90s!) There is currently no cure for dementia and to many it can seem like a death sentence, but there are those who are seriously challenging that idea.

Studies are now suggesting that simple mental exercises can transform the lives of people with dementia because they challenge and stimulate the brain and can even slow down memory loss – one of the classic symptoms of the disease.

The findings of a study recently published in the journal JAMA Internal Medicine (the international peer-reviewed journal providing innovative and clinically relevant research for practitioners in general internal medicine), indicate that the proportion of elderly people developing dementia in the US is falling, backing up similar findings in the UK and Europe.

Data from 21,057 people over the age of 65 in the US showed the proportion with dementia fell from 11.6% in 2000 to 8.8% in 2012. Similar studies in Europe, published in the Lancet Neurology last year, also suggested dementia rates had fallen in the UK and had stabilised in other European countries.

The US study, conducted at the University Of Michigan, showed that the longer the study participants had spent in education, the better their chances of fending off dementia. Seemingly, the mental challenge of learning a new subject or skill helps protect brain cells from dying later in life, or that once neurons start to die, education helps the rest of the brain rewire and compensate to prevent the symptoms of dementia appearing. To me, these results underline the need to keep our minds mentally active and stimulated throughout our lives.

Physical exercise can also help stimulate the brain and keep it healthy. Other research at the University of British Columbia discovered very recently that regular aerobic exercise – the type that literally gets your heart, lungs and sweat glands pumping faster than normal – appears to boost the size of the hippocampus, the area of the brain that controls memory. This finding comes at a critical time because, at the time of writing, one new case of dementia is detected every four seconds globally. At the present rate, *without a cure*, that means by 2050, there will be more than 115 million sufferers worldwide. Having said that, however, Professor Kenneth Langa, who conducted the University of Michigan study said: "Our results add to a growing body of evidence that this decline in dementia risk is a real phenomenon, and that the expected future growth in the burden of dementia may not be as extensive as once thought." I find that very encouraging.

Exercise reduces insulin resistance and inflammation and stimulates the release of chemicals that have a positive effect on brain cells and the growth of new blood vessels.

Exercise can also improve sleep patterns and reduce stress and anxiety. The best evidence suggests sleep serves a couple of key roles, namely in memory consolidation and muscle repair. During sleep, the brain flushes away random information and just retains important 'data.' It reasons there is no need to remember, for example, each email you deleted that day or what the registration number was on the car ahead of you in traffic. A busy day can also leave the body tired. Sleep helps replenish hormones and repair muscles.

Missing sleep robs the body of these functions. Sleep-deprived brains are, on average, smaller in volume and less populous in brain cells. Again, recent studies uphold the idea that well-rested brains are the healthiest brains.

So how much sleep do we need?

The National Sleep Foundation in the US recently recruited 18 leading scientists and researchers to update official guidelines. They based their recommendations on over 300 scientific publications and took into account the health benefits and also the risks, associated with sleep. Too little sleep over several nights leaves you tired (obviously!), unable to concentrate and depressed. Paradoxically, too much sleep can deliver the same problems.

The published guidelines recognise that sleep needs vary across ages and are impacted by lifestyle and health, but the rule of thumb recommendations are shown in this chart:

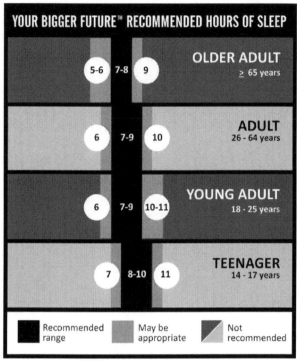

National Sleep Foundation guidelines

And what about food? Does what we eat and drink have any effect on the condition of our brains? Yes it does, according to research. Remember when your Gran told you that fish was good for your brain? Well it turns out she was right. Another recent study conducted by Professor Welma Stonehouse of Massey University in New Zealand has demonstrated that a diet which includes oily fish can boost memory function by 15%. The study examined, over a six month period, 176 healthy adults who were given supplements containing DHA, an Omega 3 fatty acid found in salmon, mackerel, sardines, trout, prawns and mussels. DHA is one of the most highly concentrated fats in the brain and known to play a vital role in its function. However, the brain cannot effectively produce DHA itself, so it has to be consumed as part of a diet.

The results were compared with those of a placebo group of volunteers. It was discovered that the memory and speed of recall of all 176 showed significant improvement. (The NHS recommends that a healthy diet should include at least two portions of fish a week, including one of oily fish.)

On the flip side, another study showed that obesity, the scourge of the developed world, can contribute to an increased risk of Alzheimer's at an earlier age. Dr. Madhav Thambisetty of America's National Institute on Ageing has reported that maintaining a healthy body mass index (BMI), a measure of weight to height, during mid-life is likely to have long-lasting protective effects. *(A NHS chart showing recommended height / weight ratios is reproduced in the previous chapter, 'A Healthy Body.')* His information comes from the Baltimore Longitudinal Study of Aging, one of the longest-running projects to track what happens to healthy people as they get older. They studied nearly 1,400 participants who had undergone regular cognitive testing every year or two for about 14 years; 142 of them developed Alzheimer's.

The researchers checked how much those Alzheimer's patients weighed when they were 50 and still cognitively healthy. Every step up on the BMI chart predicted that when Alzheimer's eventually struck, it would be 6 ½ months sooner. What this means is that, among this group of Alzheimer's patients, someone who had been obese - a BMI of 30 during middle age – on average had their dementia strike about a year earlier than someone whose midlife BMI was 28. The threshold for being overweight is a BMI of 25.

Some of the study participants underwent brain scans during life and autopsies at death. Those tests found people with higher midlife BMIs also had more of the brain-clogging hallmarks of Alzheimer's (clumps of beta-amyloid proteins, known as plaque) years later, even if they didn't develop dementia.

And here's another revelation. Well... maybe not such a revelation! Excessive alcohol consumption can be harmful to the brain. It's not called 'the silent killer' for nothing. Whilst alcohol can have a temporary positive impact on mood, in the long term it has been linked to a range of issues including depression and memory loss. The fact is, alcohol alters the brain chemistry. Time for another medico-scientific explanation. Bear with me.

Our brains rely on a delicate balance of chemicals and processes. Alcohol is a depressant, which means it can disrupt that balance, affecting our thoughts, feelings and actions – and sometimes our long-term mental health. This is partly down to 'neurotransmitters', chemicals that help to transmit signals from one nerve (or neuron) in the brain to another.

The relaxed feeling induced by that first drink is due to the chemical changes alcohol has caused in the brain. For many of us, a drink can help us feel more confident and less anxious. That's because it's starting to depress the part of the brain we associate with inhibition.

As more alcohol is consumed, so more of the brain starts to be affected. When high levels of alcohol are involved, instead of pleasurable effects increasing, it's possible that a negative emotional response will take over. It can induce anger, aggression, anxiety or depression.

Soon after drinking alcohol, brain processes slow down and memory can be impaired. After large quantities of alcohol, the brain can stop recording into the 'memory store', causing short-term memory failure or 'black outs.' This doesn't necessarily mean that brain cells have been damaged, but frequent heavy sessions *can* damage the brain because of alcohol's effect on brain chemistry and processes. Drinking heavily over a long period of time can also have long-term effects on memory. Even on days without alcohol, recalling events of yesterday, or even earlier that day, become difficult.

Drinkaware (https://www.drinkaware.co.uk) is an alcohol education charity which publishes the UK's Chief Medical Officer's guidelines for safe alcohol consumption. It recommends no more than 14 units a week for both men and women.

So it's important to remember that many of the supposed age-related changes which affect the mind, such as memory loss, are lifestyle-related. Just as muscles get flabby from doing nothing, so does the brain.

A healthy mind will help you find your way through life and a positive mental attitude will lead to a greater sense of wellbeing and a sense of purpose.

Here then are 10 generally recommended steps towards a healthy mind:

1. Eat healthily: A healthy body makes a healthy mind. Think carefully about your diet and what foods you maybe eat too much of. As I said previously, the old adage 'You are what you eat,' rings true.

2. Monitor what alcohol you drink: Just three pieces of advice – moderation, moderation, moderation.

3. Physical exercise: You don't have to go to a gym – anything that raises your heart rate – walking, cycling, gardening – something that makes you perspire.

4. Mental exercise: Put that calculator away. Work it out in your head like you used to! Learn a new word every day. Challenge your mind.

5. Engage with others: It's never been easier to keep in touch with friends and family. Strong relationships will make you feel connected.

6. Change scenery: Take a holiday by all means, but it can be as simple as taking a different route to work. Break your day-to-day routines.

7. Learn to relax: Read, walk, paint, meditate. Whatever works for you! Why not attend a mindfulness class?

8. Widen your interests: A new hobby, maybe. Learn a new skill or language. Do something you've always wanted to do.

9. Be confident: You are as good as anyone else and you are unique. Make yourself the best person you can be.

10. Care for others: Show concern and compassion for other peoples' welfare. Always treat others as you would wish to be treated yourself. You may rediscover feelings you've grown out of touch with.

HEALTHY MIND QUICK START TIPS

1. Decide on your goals. Use the ready-made template *Your Bigger Future™ Achievable Goals* template (available at the end of this book). Tell people about them. That way you've made a commitment!
2. Be patient! You've spent your whole life getting where you are today. You won't be able to change overnight. Give yourself 12 months to get to the 'new you.'
3. Continually remind yourself of the things that boost your confidence. Use the ready-made template *Your Bigger Future™ Confidence Booster* (available at the end of this book).
4. You know if you have bad habits. Change them! Use the ready-made template *Your Bigger Future™ Habit Adjuster* (available at the end of this book).
5. Take time to reflect on your progress with a regular journal. Use the ready-made template *Your Bigger Future™ Journal* (available at the end of this book).

TAILPIECE: INSPIRATION

Roger Bannister was the first person to run a mile in under four minutes. He achieved this feat with minimal training – whilst practicing as a junior doctor! It took a sense of extreme certainty for him to do what many commentators considered impossible, but on 6 May 1954, he realised his goal, setting a new world record of 3 minutes 59.4 seconds, with fellow runners Chris Chataway and Chris Brasher providing the pacing.

Roger Bannister went on to become a distinguished neurologist, Master of Pembroke College, Oxford and the first Chairman of the Sports Council. He initiated the first testing for use of anabolic steroids in sport and was knighted in 1975.

When asked 50 years after the event whether he considered the sub-four minute mile to be the greatest achievement of his life, Bannister replied to the effect that no, he considered his subsequent work as a neurologist and the procedures he introduced, as being more significant.

The man who can drive himself further once the effort gets painful is the man who will win.

Sir Roger Gilbert Bannister CBE

THOUGHT FOR THE DAY: HEALTHY MIND

What have I done, or will I do, to boost my confidence - yesterday / today / tomorrow?

5 HEALTHY PERSONAL FINANCES

5 HEALTHY PERSONAL FINANCES

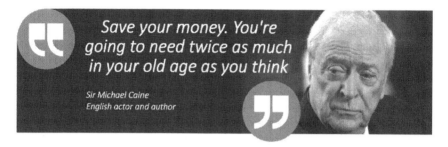

> *Save your money. You're going to need twice as much in your old age as you think*
>
> Sir Michael Caine
> English actor and author

I'm a financial consultant. I've spent my working life encouraging people to articulate their hopes and aspirations for the future and then helping them put in place a financial plan to potentially realise those goals. It's a very satisfying and rewarding job.

My clients range from those of moderate means to the very wealthy. But do you know, I've come to realise over the years that the concept of wealth is relative. Whether you have modest savings or are a multi-millionaire, you are likely to share the same fears and misgivings, albeit at varying levels of concern. Will I have enough money to last my lifetime?

Now that we can look forward to the prospect of spending upwards of a third of our lives 'in retirement' – a time when we are no longer earning money from an occupation – these concerns are tending to increase.

Our parents and grandparents by and large did not have those worries. They retired at the ages of 60 and 65 and hoped to survive, if they were lucky, another 10 or 15 years. (My own grandparents all died in their early 70s.) All their lives they'd had to be careful managing what they had and the state pension sufficed in their later years.

How times have changed! Lifespans have increased – a trend which I am convinced will continue exponentially – whilst the value of the state pension *(UK)* has decreased in real terms. There is no doubt that living longer and making money last is a real dilemma for many and this is borne out by extensive research and surveys. Perhaps not unexpectedly, many people are also as worried about the here-and-now as they are about the future. Evidence from the Citizens Advice Bureau and other organisations in the UK shows that, across the whole income spectrum, people are concerned that they may not even have enough money left at the end of the week or month to buy essentials! They are also worried about debt and the rising cost of living. Around half of all those surveyed admitted to agonising regularly about whether or not they'll have enough money for their family's future, with education, savings and pensions topping the list of concerns.

All this is enough to ensure that one in seven UK adults lose sleep over these issues. And we all know that lack of sleep can cause its own problems. It can affect the ability to concentrate, get work done and stay alert during the day. It can impact on relationships and it produces an emotional burden which in turn can lead to frustration, helplessness and loneliness.

It is said that in the USA, half the population will run out of money before the age of 80 and in Australia, half will run out just 15 years into retirement.

It seems therefore that worrying over money is the biggest stress factor in life for a large percentage of the population. This is not conducive to a healthy mind and a healthy body and there's a real danger it could undermine the prospect of embracing and enjoying Your Bigger Future™.

The concerns raised by my clients that their money would run out during their lifetimes was one of the catalysts that set me off on the journey to write this book and help others plan for their futures. Their concerns also made me realise that conventional financial planning was an outdated model. Today, I think financial planning should be easy to understand, adaptable to changing circumstances, accommodating and visionary. We all want to live comfortably now, of course, but we need to think much further ahead – not just in terms of years, but decades.

We would all like to be wealthy. But what does 'being wealthy' actually mean? To me it means being able to afford to do what you want without eroding your capital. So regular income is the key to maintaining your chosen lifestyle. And income can only be derived from a capital resource or asset that you have built up or acquired during your life with a view to securing a financially sound future. It really is all about prudence, sound financial advice and forward thinking.

It may be worth reiterating here the need to look after your physical and mental health. It's all very well working really hard to build up wealth, but make sure that at the end of the day you are still as fit as possible to enjoy the rewards of your toil. The costs of long term care are rising steadily and you won't want to see your wealth whittled away before your very eyes. The longer you can keep this at bay the better! British insurer LV recently conducted research which showed that over the last decade, the average length of stay in a care home was around two years, seven months, costing about £75,000 per person. This figure is higher than the average pension fund! So how are these costs being met? Well, LV's study also highlighted the fact that 22% of retirees had to sell their homes and 38% used their savings, to cover care costs. Those adults with parents in care often have to dig into their own pockets to support them.

So the key to healthy finances is to build up enough capital to provide the required level of income you need to sustain you during your working life and beyond when you either can't or don't want to work. Bear in mind that your income needs will almost certainly change during your retirement years. As your requirements and goals constantly shift, the income you want can be represented by the so-called 'Smile' curve...

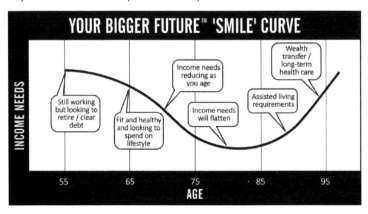

73

In the companion website to this book www.yourbiggerfuture.co.uk you will find a Capital and Income Calculator that can provide an indication of the level of income you'll need to sustain your lifestyle in retirement.

On retirement, you may have many (possibly expensive!) aspirations to fulfil. You may even have a 'bucket list,' which I cover in Chapter 9. But as you age, your spending will tend to become less each year as you achieve your ambitions, have fewer outgoings or become less able. And then, in your later years you may experience poor health that could require external, paid help or even a move to a residential care facility. So your income needs will increase once again – a modern phenomenon.

What I'm really saying is that it's OK to spend money in retirement – after all, isn't that what we aim for during our working lives? But we also need to be circumspect. Sustainability and an eye to the future should always be a key consideration.

You may spend your working life as an employee or you may become a business owner and entrepreneur. But whichever path you choose the challenge to build capital will be similar. Your motivation and responsibilities will differ of course but at the end of the day you'll want to provide for yourself and your family, now and in the future. If you run, or help run a company, you'll be helping provide for the future of others too, so you'll want the business to flourish and become a valuable asset in your financial portfolio.

Financial matters can be complex and decisions difficult to make, even for the well informed. A simple approach is needed and it may be helpful to talk separately about individual finances and business finances, although neither are mutually exclusive of course as business owners are also individuals! So this chapter will concentrate on Personal Finances. Business Finances follow in the next chapter.

■■

How do we make the most of our personal money? With normal daily expenditure and the demands of modern living – mortgages, children's education, holidays and so on, how can we build a capital resource for our later lives?

Increasing longevity means we'll probably need twice as much money as the previous generations to sustain us. It's a fact that today's older generation is by and large better off than their parents. The so-called 'Baby Boomers' (those born between 1946 and 1965) and 'Generation X' (those born between 1966 and 1980) have enjoyed higher incomes, cheaper housing and lower inflation than the 'Millennials' (those born between 1981 and 2000).

Research published in July 2016 by the Resolution Foundation (a non-partisan think-tank that conducts authoritative, analytical research into UK living standards), suggests that 'Millennials' risk becoming the first ever generation to earn less in relative terms than their predecessors over the course of their working lives.

In the UK, many of today's older generation have benefitted from Defined Benefit (DB) pension schemes, underwritten by governments and employers – that is, pensions based on final salaries and linked to inflation. An ageing population and changing workforce make such schemes unworkable today. DB schemes have been largely replaced with Defined Contribution (DC) arrangements that rely on employee savings, employer contributions and investments to build up a pension fund. In other words, the individual now has to assume the risk of securing his or her retirement income. Recent UK auto-enrolment legislation has gone a long way towards persuading today's workers and employers to make pension provision, but it is not a panacea and may not prove entirely adequate in the long term.

British insurer Royal London forecasts that today's workforce may be forced to work into their late seventies and beyond if they want to enjoy the same level of pension as their parents' generation. Their study was based on those contributing the minimum pension contributions required under the auto-enrolment legislation. It found that someone on average earnings targeting the 'gold standard' of a total pension of two thirds of their pre-retirement income, and securing inflation protection and provision for a surviving spouse, would need to work to age 77. Someone targeting the 'silver standard' of half their pre-retirement income would need to work to just over age 71.

Both cases are based on someone starting to save at age 22 and continuing to contribute each and every year until they retire.

Those who start saving at 35 need to work to 79 for a "gold standard" pension with index-linking and provision for widows and widowers, while those who delay starting to save until 45 would have to work into their eighties to make up the shortfall!

Another recent survey by insurer Prudential indicated that many workers believe they will be underfunded for retirement and will be unable to afford to retire.

As I see it then, unless retirement is to become a 'luxury' enjoyed by the few, with many being forced to work much longer than they'd wish, the onus of building sufficient capital rests entirely with us as individuals. The UK State pension in the future is unlikely to provide anything other than a basic level of comfort.

It may seem obvious, but there are some basic rules to follow when managing your income and capital.

- Build it up
- Look after it
- Ensure it doesn't run out
- Use all the tax breaks available to you
- Invest wisely – do it yourself if you feel capable or seek professional advice
- Ensure your residual capital and assets are passed to your beneficiaries in the most tax-efficient way possible

There are three principle areas I would recommend you address from the very beginning to lay solid foundations for a lifetime financial strategy. You should make contingency plans for these circumstances:

1. If you fall sick, injured or become ill
2. If you die prematurely
3. If you live to a ripe old age!

Clearly the first two scenarios require insurance to be put into place, not only to protect you, but your family also. A professional consultant will help you ensure the right cover is in place or you can visit one of the many comparison sites available online. Helpful web site suggestions are also available on the companion web site www.yourbiggerfuture.co.uk .

The third contingency? Well that's really what this chapter is about. Providing the ongoing income and capital resource to ensure financial comfort for Your Bigger Future™. Again, the advice of a professional consultant could prove invaluable to help you achieve your goals if you need help.

Although good advice is available, it is now not quite so readily accessible as it has been in the past. Recent changes in remits and stringent examination requirements have made the modern UK financial consultant career uber-professional. That's excellent news for the general public, but paradoxically has made access to that advice rather more difficult. The reason for this is two-fold. It has meant that the number of practicing consultants has drastically decreased, whilst the population – and therefore, in theory, the number of those seeking advice – has steadily increased, leading to an 'advice gap.'

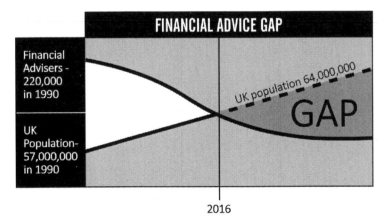

This, coupled with the fact that consultants no longer receive commission on investment products and have to charge a fee means that a new generation of online-based, non-advised guidance services, suitable for investors who know enough about financial services to invest on a DIY basis, are springing up to help bridge the gap. But of course nothing beats sitting down and talking to a professional consultant who will be able to take your personal circumstances into account, particularly if those circumstances are complex.

Addressing our third contingency – securing income and capital for our later years – is not entirely straightforward as many factors and life events can get in the way of our plans at any time during our lives. It's more manageable if we break down our requirements into distinct time periods.
1. Short term
2. Medium term
3. Long term

Easy to say, of course. A little harder to put into practice, maybe. I think it's more achievable if you can clearly visualise the things you'll want and need. Categorise them and build funds for each. As an example, an outline plan for someone living in the UK could look like this:

YOUR BIGGER FUTURE™ PLANNED EXPENDITURE

TIME FRAME	EVENT	AMOUNT NEEDED	DATE NEEDED	HOW FUNDED	NOTES
Short Term *	New car	£5,000	2 years	Savings account with bank, building society, or ISA	All allow quick and ready access
	Holidays	£3,000	1 year		
	Frivolities	£2,000	3 years		
Medium Term**	Moving house	£20,000	10 years	ISA / General Investment Account	Only one ISA allowed per person (husband / wife / partner can have one each)
	Major family holiday	£20,000	10 years		
	Childrens' education	£25,000	5 - 10 years		
Long Term***	Retirement	£500,000	30 years	Pension	Many different types of pension, private and company
	Help children buy first home	£50,000	30 years	ISA / Bond / General Investment Account	
	'Leave work' fund	£100,000	30 years		

* Short Term: 1 - 2 years   ** Medium Term: 2 - 10 years   *** Long Term: 10 years +

You'll obviously have your own agenda, but I'm sure you get the picture.

Additionally you may find it helpful to split and allocate your income broadly along these lines:

YOUR BIGGER FUTURE™ PERSONAL FINANCES

INCOME	
1/3	**Financial goals** Medium / long term savings and investments for anticipated and unexpected life events, such as moving home, retirement, long term care.
1/3	**Fixed costs** Items such as utilities, car payments, the mortgage, regular subscriptions (e.g. TV and gym membership).
1/3	**Flexible spending** Everyday living expenses that may vary, such as food, eating out, shopping, hobbies, entertainment, fuel.

(Blank templates can be found at the end of this book or downloaded from www.yourbiggerfuture.co.uk)

So what level of income – how much money – do you think you'll need in retirement? That's almost like asking how long is a piece of string? 'How much is enough?' is a discussion I often have with clients. In reality though, it's a question that only you can answer.

Your spending habits will change, there's no doubt about that. You'll spend less on some things, but more on others. Swings and roundabouts. For example, you'll probably have paid off your mortgage and your children will have left home, both of which will considerably reduce your monthly outgoings. You'll save on commuting costs and of course you'll no longer need to contribute to a pension as you'll be drawing from it! But you'll need to balance those savings against the fact that your leisure expenditure on hobbies, sports and holidays may increase and your heating bills may rise if you spend more time at home. You should also bear in mind the potential costs of long-term care, either in your own home or in a residential home.

A little time spent formulating a rudimentary budget model for your retirement will prove very useful in calculating your target income and when used in conjunction with a pension and income forecast can highlight any shortfalls that need to be addressed. It makes sense to do this sooner rather than later so that you'll have more time to make up any likely deficit.

It's a fairly fundamental and straightforward exercise. You'll need say, three months' worth of bank and credit card statements (which should include information about insurance renewals, direct debits, etc.), payslips and shopping receipts and you'll need to factor in one-off spends such as birthdays, Christmas, holidays, car repairs and so on. That should give you some idea of your expenditure over a year. Next, work out where you are likely to save money in retirement and where you may spend more. This is not an exact science, but put this all in the mix and a clear picture should start to emerge of the level of income you'll ideally need to enjoy a comfortable retirement.

It may be that your overall financial requirements will not decrease significantly. That means you'll need a similar income to that enjoyed during your employment years. The UK's National Employment Savings Trust (NEST) says that £15,000 - £20,000 is the minimum annual income for which to aim to 'guarantee' a comfortable retirement. (This of course could include the approximate £7,500 per annum (at the time of writing) single tier UK state pension). That equates to the generally accepted view that most people need approximately two thirds of their working life income to live on in retirement. The average UK employment income (2016) is around £26,000 - £27,000.

To generate £26,000 income a year for all of your life, on the basis that you want to be self-sufficient and not rely on state benefits, would require an investment, pension fund or other capital asset of £650,000, returning 4% interest per annum.

For many people this could be a massive 'wake-up' call, but by now you'll have hopefully approximately calculated what you'll need to live on in retirement. To estimate your own position go to www.yourbiggerfuture.co.uk and put your own details into the quick Capital and Income Calculator.

Now we'll explore how you can build the capital that will provide the income you need per annum for the rest of your life to accommodate Your Bigger Future™.

There are a million and one ways to invest for capital growth and build up your money. Most of them require an in-depth knowledge of the area you choose to be in to stand any chance of making money. There are some that are reasonably solid bets if you know what you are doing, such as property, fine wines, antiques and vintage/classic cars. The drawback is that you'll need substantial funds to start with and like any speculative venture, nothing is certain in this world and you may end up with less value than your original investment.

I will confine my comments then to traditional, financial investments, based on my knowledge and experience built up during my career in the

UK financial services business spanning over 40 years. Bear in mind this will be generic, non-technical guidance as everyone's personal circumstances, attitude to risk and goals are different. *Also please understand that my comments are based around financial products and the tax regime (2017/18) current in the UK and will differ depending on your particular country of residence.*

Financial investment simply means putting aside an amount of money, either as a lump sum or in instalments and expecting a gain from it within a chosen time frame. The aim, in this context, is to help ensure your investment and retirement goals are realised so that you can enjoy Your Bigger Future™ without having to worry about money.

There are two components to an investment – the product itself (often referred to as the 'tax wrapper') and the way it is invested. Tax efficiency is the key because it is clearly much easier to build capital in a non-taxed, tax-exempt or tax-efficient environment than out of taxed income. In my view, there are five main UK investment vehicles worth considering:

- Pensions
- Individual Savings Accounts (ISAs)
- Life Assurance Bonds
- Personal Portfolios, unit trusts and shares
- Cash deposits

Here are the main features:

- **Pensions**

Based on your personal circumstances and income, the maximum you can invest into a pension is £40,000 a year. High incomes may be subject to a tapering of this Annual Allowance down to £10,000. The contributions attract tax relief at the basic rate of tax (20%). In other words, if you are a basic rate taxpayer and contribute £8,000 into your pension, the tax man adds £2,000 to make a total investment of £10,000. Higher or additional rate tax payers can claim back even more via their self-assessment tax returns. If you are not earning in the tax year or earn less than £3,600 you can still contribute up to £3,600 into your pension and receive tax relief at the basic rate.

➢ **Advantages:**
1. Basic rate tax relief on premiums and reclaim of additional tax via self-assessment
2. Potential for employer contributions
3. Tax-free growth in the fund
4. 25% tax-free cash withdrawal benefit after age 55
5. Inheritance Tax (IHT) efficient as uncrystallised funds remain out of your estate for IHT purposes

➢ **Disadvantages:**
1. No access to benefits before age 55
2. Annual Allowance and Lifetime Allowance caps
3. Income in retirement taxed as earned income at your highest marginal rate
4. Product charges
5. Tax credit paid with dividends can't be reclaimed
6. Investments can fall as well as rise

For more information on UK pensions, visit:
https://www.pensionsadvisoryservice.org.uk/about-pensions

• **New Individual Savings Accounts (NISAs)**
The maximum individual contribution is £20,000 a year from April 2017, which can be invested in either cash or stocks and shares (S&S), or a combination of both.

➢ **Advantages:**
1. Tax-efficient (S&S) and tax-free (Cash) growth in the fund
2. Tax-free on withdrawal
3. Free of Capital Gains Tax (CGT) on disposal
4. Access to capital at any time
5. Spouses / Civil Partners receive an additional NISA allowance equal to the value of their Spouse's or Civil Partner's NISA savings at the time of their death

➢ **Disadvantages:**
1. Annual Allowance
2. Product charges
3. Investments can fall as well as rise (S&S)
4. If you withdraw money from your NISA, you don't reset your annual limit

For more information visit:
https://www.moneyadviceservice.org.uk/en/articles/stocks-and-shares-isas

A new Lifetime ISA (LISA) is available from April 2017 for those aged between 18 and 40 years of age. Savers can put up to £4,000 a year into the LISA. Then the state will add a 25% bonus of tax relief on top, making a total contribution of £5,000. And that's before interest or growth. Any money you put into your Lifetime ISA will be included as part of your annual ISA contribution limit. The money is to be used either towards a first home worth under £450,000 or, once you are over 60, towards retirement. However, if you use this money for anything other than home purchase, or before age 60, there is a 25% withdrawal penalty.

For more information visit:
http://www.moneysavingexpert.com/savings/lifetime-ISAs

• **Life Assurance Bond**
A little used but very tax efficient, simple product with no limit on how much can be invested! You can withdraw up to 5% of your original investment a year for up to 20 years, which is tax deferred until the bond is cashed, and does not need to be declared on your tax return. If you don't use your 5% allowance in a given year, the allowance is carried over to the following year. All gains and income earned within an investment bond are taxed at 20%.

➢ **Advantages:**
1. Beneficial tax treatment as fund grows
2. 5% tax-efficient withdrawals a year

3. Can be written in trust so that the investment can be passed on tax-efficiently to family
4. Available as an onshore or offshore investment
5. Can switch between funds without creating a taxable gain
6. Any taxable element (i.e. over 5% p.a.) can be treated as savings income where there is available a separate annual allowance
7. Can be clustered /segmented for tax-efficiency

➢ **Disadvantages:**
1. May not be suitable for non-taxpayers
2. Can be complicated from a tax position
3. 5% withdrawals will be added to any profit made and taxed as income in the tax year in which the bond is disposed of
4. There may be surrender penalties in the early years
5. Professional advice may be needed
6. Investments can fall as well as rise

For more information visit:
https://www.moneyadviceservice.org.uk/en/articles/investment-bonds

• **Personal Portfolios / Unit Trusts / Shares**
Invest any amount, but Capital Gains Tax (CGT) will potentially apply upon disposal. You have a CGT Annual Allowance of £11,100.

➢ **Advantages:**
1. Annual CGT Allowance
2. Dividend allowance of £5,000 per annum
3. Flexible and accessible
4. Transparent and easy to see underlying investments
5. No limit on the investment amount

➢ **Disadvantages:**
1. Switching between funds potentially creates a taxable gain
2. Potentially many different fees and charges to pay
3. Investments can fall as well as rise
4. Higher risks depending on the sector/stock/fund chosen

For more information visit:
https://www.moneyadviceservice.org.uk/en/articles/popular-investments-at-a-glance

- **Cash Deposits / Instant Access Savings Accounts**

There are many different deposit and savings accounts with banks and building societies available on the high street. It is advisable to shop around for the best returns as these change from time to time. A new personal savings allowance of £1,000 was introduced in April 2016, removing the first £1,000 of savings income from income tax. Higher rate taxpayers benefit from a smaller personal savings allowance of £500. Additional rate taxpayers have no allowance.

➢ **Advantages:**
1. Lower risk and very accessible
2. Non tax payers can ask for interest to be paid without any tax deductions
3. Usually no charges

➢ **Disadvantages**
1. Potentially very low interest rates
2. Taxed at basic rate. If you are a higher, or additional rate tax payer then this will be covered under your self-assessment tax return
3. Some accounts have early withdrawal penalties

For more information visit;
https://www.moneyadviceservice.org.uk/en/search?query=cash+savings

Legislation governing the maximum amounts allowable to invest – and the tax treatments of these products – is subject to change from time to time. *(My information is based on tax allowances and my understanding of tax law current at the time of writing – 2017 /18).* There are a number of sources where you can find all the latest, up-to-date information on the UK investment tax rules. These are just two:
http://moneyfacts.co.uk/guides/money/moneyfacts-tax-table/
http://www.scottishwidows.co.uk/Extranet/Literature/Doc/SW56316

So, those are some of the products and tax allowances available to UK taxpayers. So far, so good. Those are typical investment *products*, but what about the investment *process*? This is where the skill and experience of a good financial consultant will 'pay dividends.' That's because your consultant should take into account your attitude to investment risk and capacity for loss and assemble a portfolio that reflects this and your ultimate financial goals. Where I work, we follow a tried and tested formula.

INVESTMENT PROCESS	
STAGE 1	Understanding your financial goals and objectives
STAGE 2	Establishing your attitude to risk and investment experience
STAGE 3	Tax wrapper recommendations, service levels and product providers
STAGE 4	Selecting and implementing your chosen investment solution
STAGE 5	Ongoing communication with you, reviews, and rebalancing - keeping your investments on track

It may be worth explaining a little about fund management. You may have heard the terms 'passive fund management' and 'active fund management.' Passively managed funds simply 'track' a particular market, purchase funds in that market and consequently reflect the performance of that market. Actively managed funds are run by professional fund managers allied to research teams who operate across all markets and aim to deliver returns that are superior to the market as a whole. For funds with more conservative investment strategies, the mandate will be to protect capital to mitigate losses if markets fall.

Certainly, I am a great believer in active fund management, which allows for speedy, fluid, tactical asset allocation adjustments to take account of market fluctuations and opportunities. The key is to make sure you choose an active fund manager that will consistently make the right calls. Again, the counsel of a good financial consultant will be of huge advantage when making your choice.

What I'm advocating is for you to look to the medium to long term. That's what investment and retirement planning is all about. I have a favourite graph which illustrates that over an extended period, the trend is for growth in the long term, because investments follow a distinct pattern. The lean times of market volatility and stagnation, typically lasting 15 – 20 years, are invariably followed by periods of sustained growth.

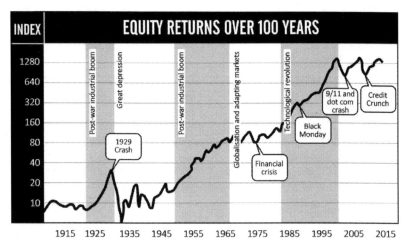

Graph based on US Equity market as this is the longest data available. Total returns, inflation adjusted.
Source: Reuters Ecowin / Prof. Robert Schiller, Yale University
Past performance should not be relied on as a guarantee of future performance

I therefore believe it's a great idea to develop an ongoing relationship and dialogue with a financial consultant so that your changing circumstances can be monitored and your investments adjusted accordingly.

However, I understand that not everyone is in a position to pay for financial advice and for smaller investments it might not be cost effective in any event. As I mentioned previously there are a number of internet sites which cater for self-investment and there is a plethora of financial information available via search engines that can guide you. You can find out more about this at www.yourbiggerfuture.co.uk .

You may wish to consider utilising the capital value of your house to provide extra funds. Equity release allows you to access this asset either as a lump sum or in regular smaller amounts. Clearly the income provider will need to be recompensed at a later date, usually on your demise. The drawback, in addition to being complicated, is that there will be less value – or indeed none at all – in your home to pass to beneficiaries.

And that brings me to other considerations that I strongly recommend you address at some stage – making a Will and Inheritance Tax (IHT) issues. A Will will ensure that your legacy is distributed according to your wishes and tackling IHT can mitigate any tax liability. Without wishing to repeat myself, solid financial advice is invaluable when considering IHT as it is a very complicated subject with many pitfalls for the unwary. An online calculator to provide an indication of your IHT liability can be found at www.yourbiggerfuture.co.uk .

Those with substantial wealth can still entertain fears that they will not have enough money to sustain themselves, or indeed a particular lifestyle, in later years. I am minded of a client, a high earning CEO of a national company. During her career she had accumulated no less than seven separate pensions but had no idea of their worth or whether they would provide enough income in retirement. It was possible to consolidate all her pensions into one fund and I provided a cash flow profiler to illustrate the potential income this asset could deliver. This allayed her long held concerns and relieved the stress that she had felt for many years.

But there is another side to the coin. There are those who know exactly how much they are worth, but then choose to spend money... shall we say, unwisely. Another personal client, having built up a very successful company sold out to a larger organisation for a very substantial sum. He then went on a spending spree that ended in tears. He bought a very nice barn conversion but failed to insure it. It burnt down! He bought a property 'off plan' in Portugal just before the developer went bankrupt!

He then bought two office buildings intent on converting them to dwellings but failed to secure planning permission! Luckily he retained his home but had to start another business to rebuild his capital and provide income for daily living.

Another client built a successful business and sold it to a national company. The proceeds allowed him to retire abroad in his mid-fifties. He assumed his capital would be sufficient for the rest of his life. Not so. He had to return to work in his mid-sixties to provide an income!

The moral of these three true accounts is to know the exact worth of your assets and 'ring fence' the amount you will need to fund your retirement income in perpetuity. You can estimate the projected income from your investment and pension fund and identify any shortfall, without engaging a consultant, by utilising one of the many free calculators available on the internet or the Capital and Income Calculator on the companion web site, www.yourbiggerfuture.co.uk

Here then are my top tips that will help you towards securing a sound financial basis for your retirement:

- Start saving as early as possible. Even saving just £10 a month from an early age will, with the benefit of compound interest, realise a healthy return in later years
- Make a plan and regularly review it
- Ensure your investments are tailored to your personal attitude to risk and capacity for loss
- Use all the tax breaks available to you. It's more financially efficient to build your wealth from gross income and in tax-efficient investments
- Arrange for all your savings, assets and investments to be summarised in one place.
- Make a Will that reflects your wishes rather than leaving this to chance!
- Perform a cash flow profile, using the Capital and Income Calculator on our companion web site, www.yourbiggerfuture.co.uk

- If you need help – seek it! You can get free information about how to choose a financial consultant in the UK from
The Pensions Advisory Service
(www.pensionsadvisoryservice.org.uk), or
The Money Advice Service
(www.moneyadviceservice.org.uk)

I must reiterate that the information I have provided in this chapter does not constitute financial advice or specific recommendations and therefore does not form part of any contract for the sale or purchase of an investment. Should you wish to consider investing you should initially read the Key Facts documents pertaining to the products. Also, please understand that investments can carry risk and their value can fall as well as rise. In fact, you may not get back the amount you originally invested.

HEALTHY PERSONAL FINANCES QUICK START TIPS

1. Calculate the income you will need going forward into Your Bigger Future™ and the capital required to fund it (Capital and Income Calculator available at www.yourbiggerfuture.co.uk)
2. Plan your future expenditure and allocate your finances accordingly. Use the ready-made templates *Your Bigger Future™ Planned Expenditure and Your Bigger Future™ Personal Finances* (available at the end of this book).
3. Seek professional financial advice if you need it so that you can maximise your tax allowances and keep track of your investments.
4. Make a Will! Ensure your legacies will be allocated according to your wishes.
5. Insure yourself against ill health. Protect your family.

TAILPIECE: INSPIRATION

The story of author J K Rowling is probably one of the best known 'rags to riches' stories of modern times. She progressed from living on state benefits to multi-millionaire status within just five years.

After suffering from clinical depression, going through a divorce, been barely able to feed her baby and having had her first Harry Potter manuscript rejected dozens of times, she was finally accepted by a small London publisher, Bloomsbury.

Since then she has completed seven fantastically successful books in the Harry Potter series and was awarded an OBE for services to children's literature. She continues to write for adults, sometimes under the pseudonym, Robert Galbraith.

Her books have sold over 400 million copies worldwide and she has amassed an estimated fortune of £560 million.

Whatever money you might have, self-worth really lies in finding out what you do best.

J K Rowling

THOUGHT FOR THE DAY: HEALTHY PERSONAL FINANCES

What have I done, or will I do, to make, or save, money - yesterday / today / tomorrow?

6 HEALTHY BUSINESS FINANCES

6 HEALTHY BUSINESS FINANCES

> Don't be afraid to take
> a big step. You can't cross
> a chasm in two small jumps
>
> David Lloyd George
> British politician, statesman and
> Prime Minister

If you run, or help run, a business, or intend to start a business, this section is for you.

I hope I'm not being immodest when I say I have helped build a successful company in the very competitive and highly regulated arena of financial services. There are those working in the industry who may feel that we've succeeded *despite* the regulation, that ultra-regulation impedes and restricts business, but I take a different view. After all, clients entrust us with their hard-earned money and I believe it is incumbent on us to do the best we can to help protect and grow their financial investment and indeed, repay their investment in us as consultants. With trust comes great responsibility and in that respect tighter regulation can only be a good thing. But it's not been plain sailing.

Perhaps I'm stating the obvious when I say that building a successful, *profitable*, business is not easy. I could trot out all the old clichés about minefields, pitfalls and weathering the storm and so on and I have to say I've experienced my fair share of those. But over the years I have been fortunate and privileged to meet many business owners – from one-man-band, self-employed operators to the directors and CEOs of SMEs (small-to-medium enterprises) and large national and international companies – and the knowledge and insight I have gleaned along the way about how to run a successful business has proved invaluable. It's been a fascinating journey.

One thing I have learned is that, whatever the size of the enterprise, there are common themes and similarities when it comes to the fundamentals of building a healthy, prosperous, profitable company. And at the end of the day – and certainly in the context of this chapter – improving your financial bottom line with a view to Your Bigger Future™ is what it's all about.

I have to say here and now that if you already have a great business model I would not have the temerity to tell you how to run your company. What I hope is that you may find that some of the tips and knowledge I have gained from others could make your business stronger. And if you operate a young, or start-up company, they may help you hit the ground running.

What constitutes a good business? How can that business be sustained? In my experience, there are a number of vital, key areas that should be addressed to help ensure business success and profitability. Most may seem obvious and straightforward, but I can assure you that in practice, they are not and in fact many are often completely overlooked or given scant regard. However I am convinced that if you follow these principles consistently, you will succeed.

The Principles for Success in Business

1. **Build a relevant business.** Make sure you are providing what people want.

2. **Develop a clear business plan.** Three years is a good basis but be prepared to adjust the set of your sails to the prevailing wind!

3. **Have a clear vision of your target clientele and audience.** Keep focused on your market, look after existing clients and always look for new customers.

4. **Maintain a strong leadership.** Staff and clients need the reassurance that 'those at the top' know what they are doing!

5. **Make it profitable.** Know the exact cost of your product and service.

6. **Increase profits.** There are three areas to address – increase turnover, increase the margins, decrease expenses.

7. **Make the business attractive and saleable.** It should be able to run without you.

8. **Keep up with the times.** If your market is getting smaller, reinvent and adjust.

9. **Be motivated.** You're the boss – always look for new ideas to improve what you do.

10. **Treat staff well.** They need to know they are valued.

11. **The right people in the right job.** No square pegs in round holes.

12. **Persistency wins the prize.** Don't be put off your chosen course.

13. **Market your products and services well.** If you don't tell people what you do, how can you expect them to buy from you?

14. **Protect the business.** Keep on top of your insurances, legal and tax affairs.

In elaborating on these principles, I use a number of examples derived from my own experiences which I am sure you will be able to apply to your own business.

1. Build a relevant business. Make sure you are providing what people want.

'If you could see through John Smith's eyes, you would buy what John Smith buys.'

That was written on a plaque hanging on the wall behind the desk of a very successful businessman I once met in Canada. The meaning is obvious. Make sure you focus on what your customer actually wants, not on what you want to sell him / her! Very often companies pressurise salespeople into pushing products that we really don't want or need. No-one appreciates being 'sold to.'

Make it personal. Certainly in my line of work, I've found that when offering services to existing or potential business clients, it's imperative I understand what makes them and their company tick before presenting solutions to them. I came across a formula – 'SWOT,' that tends to work for me. 'SWOT' stands for **S**trengths, **W**eaknesses, **O**pportunities, **T**hreats.

I begin by asking about the company's strengths (a positive start to any conversation), its weaknesses, the opportunities up ahead and any potential threats. By listening and taking notes I develop an holistic understanding of what is important to the company and most importantly, how I can tailor my products and services to reflect that. In other words, I make the glove fit the hand, not the hand fit the glove! Clients appreciate this and it separates me from the herd. A typical 'SWOT' exercise would look something like this:

YOUR BIGGER FUTURE™ 'SWOT'

STRENGTHS	WEAKNESSES	OPPORTUNITIES	THREATS
We've been in business for 10 years	We don't look after our clients very well	The marketplace is big	We are not making enough profit and if nothing changes we will go bankrupt
We have a good reputation	We have poor cash flow	We could open up a lot more business with our existing clients	Our competitors seem to be attacking some of our clients
We have loyal customers	We haven't updated our brochures and website for a long time	We have great talent within our workforce which is not fully utilised	A number of our team members are nearing 'retirement age'
We do make a profit from our 'ideal' clients	We don't seek new clients on a regular basis	We are probably overstaffed in some areas, could deploy labour better and could save money	Our main shareholding director is in poor health and is now often not at work

(A blank template can be found at the end of this book or downloaded from www.yourbiggerfuture.co.uk)

In addition to having gathered the information I need to develop my suggestions as to how I can help the client, it has the obvious benefit of focusing them on areas of his / her business that need to be addressed. Always look to add value for the client.

Sometimes, the help a client needs may be outside of my remit, but even if this is the case, I will endeavour to refer them to someone I know who can help them. Again, added value. This enhances my reputation and I invariably find that the client and introduced source will come back to me in the future. Remember – it's not only the short game you are after, but the long one too.

This is a perfect example of what I'm talking about. I once visited a potential client, a paint manufacturer based in two locations, some distance apart. I went through the 'SWOT' exercise and discovered that the over-riding concern was the need to bring both parts of the business together for economies of scale. A unit of some 100,000 square feet was required. Clearly, my normal services were not likely to figure very highly on the list of priorities. However, I introduced them to a construction company client who subsequently acquired land on their behalf and built the unit they needed. Happily, the construction company still remains a long-standing client of my firm, has referred us to other clients time and again and I like to think of them as friends. And the paint company? Yes, it subsequently became a client!

It's important to cement your client relationships (if you'll excuse the pun). Always focus on what is important to them, not on trying to grow your business at all costs.

All companies would like to experience constant growth. Some achieve this for many years, but inevitably at some stage all businesses need to take a breather, consolidate and let the dust settle before starting the next growth phase.

I well remember a national, household name insurance company that some years ago fell into this very trap. Year on year it would post superb growth figures with predictions that the following year's figures would be even better. This relentless drive became an obsession and the company lost sight of its initial business aims – to look after its clients and balance the books! Suddenly its gearing rates (the level of its debt in relation to its equity capital) became too high for its income to sustain and the company collapsed – a victim of over confidence, recklessness and sheer greed.

2. **Develop a clear business plan.** Three years is a good basis but be prepared to adjust the set of the sail to the prevailing wind!

Without clear goals your business will drift aimlessly like a rudderless ship. What are your aims? Are they truly yours, not someone else's? How much money do you want to make?

A business plan is essential whether you are starting out or taking stock and planning the future of an established business. It's also a pre-requisite if you are looking to borrow money from a bank, venture capital, crowd funding or the like.

If you've never written a plan before, you can get useful pointers and guidance from various sources including https://www.gov.uk/write-business-plan

Essentially you should look to include the following basic elements:

Be concise
It's really important not only for you, but that potential investors can understand what your business is all about from a quick glance at your plan. Make sure you include a summary of your business, and how and by when, it will make money. Use simple language throughout.

Be specific
Being specific is just as important as being concise. The details will help you drill down into how you will actually deliver your plan.

Know your market

A big part of knowing whether your business will be successful is understanding your audience. Make sure your plan is clear about your target market – to whom will you be selling and how many other companies are already selling similar products?

Know your finances

The other essential part of a business plan is the finance section. If your business isn't going to make any money, it won't be successful so you need to be very clear on how you will make a profit. Use it to your advantage – your plan will be incredibly useful when it comes to securing loans and investment, but that's not its only use. It's also a personal tool to help you understand your objectives.

3. Have a clear vision of your target customer and audience. Keep focused on your market, look after existing customers and always look for new ones.

I have to ask. Do you have a clear picture of your ideal customer? It's not a stupid question. Some companies are not that sure, believe it or not. If you already run a company, look at your current customer base. Does it measure up to your ideal criteria and standards? If you are starting a business, can you envisage your perfect customer? If you cannot answer yes to these questions, you need to work at it. And don't forget, whilst customers are free to choose your company in the marketplace, you are equally at liberty to choose your customers. If a current or potential customer does not fit your criteria, for whatever reason, then that customer is not likely to advance your business. As my old boss used to say, "Good business is where all parties gain."

I have a set of 'Good Customer' criteria that has almost always worked for my company. A good customer will:

- Clearly communicate their needs – it's very important to know what you are expected to do

- Allow a reasonable amount of time for the work to be done - quality work takes time
- Pay a fair price for the work required – it's important to be paid properly for a good job
- Pay in a timely fashion – consistently paying late will, in time, sour a relationship
- Have high integrity – they will be honest and reliable
- Want an ongoing relationship – and repeat business is often the lowest cost to secure
- Refer you to other prospective customers
- Give credit where credit is due – they will appreciate you, your services and your products and give fair and constructive feedback

When you have your customers, make them feel important and more than just a name in your database. Keep in touch with them, using as many communication channels as you have at your disposal, to impart news and relevant messages. This also keeps your business name at the forefront of their minds.

To achieve a high level of customer satisfaction, especially in the service industries, you'll need to adhere to some pretty basic principles of etiquette.

Be on time – either when arriving at a meeting or sending a follow-up email

Keep your promises – simply do exactly what you say you will do... or try to do even more!

Finish what you start – because half a job is as bad, or worse, than no job at all

Be grateful – a 'please' and 'thank you' costs nothing. Not saying it could cost you dearly!

When dealing with larger enterprises, you'll find that frequent, key personnel changes are common. People with whom you deal are often replaced, so make sure you introduce yourself to the newbies as soon as possible, as they may have their own agenda with regard to suppliers and you won't want to be side-lined. For example, my company has provided group scheme and financial products to a very large organisation in the education services sector for over 12 years. During that time, the key members of staff – HR Directors, Group Financial Directors and CEOs – have changed many times. We have to be constantly vigilant and make it a top priority to immediately introduce ourselves to the new executives. It's not always easy, but the effort has paid off and we have retained their business.

4. Maintain a strong leadership. Staff and clients need the reassurance that 'those at the top' know what they are doing!

Whether you run a company with thousands of staff or a small business with just a handful, remember that strong, decisive, purposeful leadership is essential.

I don't believe there can be a precise definition of leadership. It could be just one characteristic or a combination of many qualities that define a leader, but it will almost certainly include enthusiasm, inspiration, guidance, direction, delegation, confidence and charisma for a strong and secure future for the company. Staff and clients alike need to feel that your business is there for the long term.

Leadership means just that. Leading from the front. Set examples that your staff can follow, such as, in my case, good business production. Then, when a member of your sales team needs support, or indeed a 'gentle push,' you are in a legitimate and authoritative position to do so. And always have a solution that can help them improve their performance. That solution of course should always include encouragement to make the best use of their own personal skills.

I tend to think of business – any business – in the context of a stage play. It shares the same basic elements.

The audience represents your clientele. The play – the entertainment – is your suite of products and services. Back stage is where the essential support functions take place, representing your office administration and preparation. And like a theatre production that runs like a well-oiled machine, so should your business. Build systems and processes and establish standard ways of doing things. Review and adjust as necessary. By doing this you can be confident that your company is running smoothly and efficiently and that time is not being wasted by your staff constantly reinventing the wheel. Equally important, your time will be freed up for creative work.

As a leader, you'll have to deal with egos. Some people's egos are bigger than others, which at times can be annoying, a real nuisance and a disruptive influence in the workplace. Well, that's human nature, but it has to be addressed. Sometimes a simple, individual 'Well done' is the right acknowledgement, whilst at other times, 'public' praise is the way to go. But be careful you don't do this in isolation. All staff achievements should be applauded.

Former American President Ronald Reagan said, "The greatest leader is not necessarily the one who does the greatest things. He is the one who gets the people to do the greatest things." Earlier, US President Harry S. Truman famously observed, "It is amazing what you can accomplish if you do not care who gets the credit."

5. Make it profitable. Know the exact cost of your product and service.

It's no good being in business just to be in business. You have to make a profit. Your company has to be, in effect, a money-making machine. That really is the bottom line and the only way to do this is to ensure your products and services are costed and sold at acceptable market rates.

Recently the UK financial services sector has been going through a period of change. Commission payment from product providers has largely been swept away, regulatory compliance costs have risen dramatically and the bar has been raised significantly with regards to industry qualification standards. So in my company we have had to rethink the way we get paid for our services. In short, we had to charge fees. The big question was – how much?

The answer was delivered to me quite suddenly and it was so simple and fundamental that it rocked me back in my seat.

I was attending my regular entrepreneurial coaching course. A Dutch delegate asked the question, "How do you avoid going bankrupt?" A few eyebrows raised in the room as the answer seemed fairly obvious. "Watch your cash flow," "Don't run out of money" and "Stay in touch with your customers" were just a few of the suggestions offered. But one delegate, a real jack-the-lad-type brimming with confidence said, "It's simple. Know the exact cost of your product and service and overheads and add 25% for your profit."

Brilliant! That was it! Right there. It wasn't rocket science. It was a 'why didn't I think of that' moment. The only consideration for me was that 25% profit would be unsustainable in my industry and a level would have to be found that was acceptable both to us as a company and to our clients.

We found that level and it's now business as usual with clearly defined profit margins. Clients *will* pay for excellent relevant products and efficient, fairly priced services.

So remember...
- Believe in your product and charge a realistic price for it
- Low inflation does not mean no inflation. Be prepared to put your prices up each year and do not attempt to absorb inflationary increases as this will whittle away your profit
- Make sure you have more money coming in than going out. Cash flow is king!

6. Increase profits. There are three areas to address – increase turnover, increase the margins, decrease expenses.

How do you increase your profits? By maintaining what you are doing, but by being smarter. Try to think laterally. Don't be afraid to adopt and adapt the ideas of others. Don't be afraid of change.

A personal client once told me that he had doubled his profits in a year. He had been working for individuals for ever, then seized an opportunity to work for a number of individuals in the same business, all at the same time, effectively grouping them together. So he was providing the same individual service but magnified several times over and at the same time cutting down on his personal travelling time and costs.

Great ideas can also come from simple observation. In late 19th century Chicago, the mass slaughter of pigs (200,000 a day) was a popular, public spectacle, believe it or not! A young Henry Ford was watching this melee one day and noticed that one man did the same task over and over again and was able to work faster and be more productive. Henry took this idea away and subsequently employed it in his car factory as the first ever production line. It was a revelation.

OK, not everyone can be an industrial revolutionary! So you could try a few basic tactics to increase your profits, such as:

Increase your prices. But be wary. You'll still need to demonstrate great value for money and there may be a price ceiling for your particular product.

Diversify. Sell other products that are complimentary to your core offering. My financial services company did this several years ago by launching an asset management sister company.

Remove the dead wood. That could include loss-making or unpopular products or even non-productive workers. (Be careful to follow human resources protocols if you have to 'let someone go.')

Negotiate better deals from your suppliers. If they won't play ball you can probably find another supplier who will.

Ask your customers for feedback to improve your offering. Ask them to be truthful, not diplomatic. Improved products mean more happy customers and more profits.

Generate new leads. Networking! Sometimes it's not what you know, but who you know. And consider online sales and services – it's increasingly the purchasing medium of choice.

7. Make the business attractive and saleable. It should be able to run without you.

Ensure that your business is attractive to potential purchasers. You may enjoy running your company and I hope you do, but you may not want to do it forever. It therefore makes perfect sense to build its capital value into a saleable entity. It also makes sense to ensure the business could carry on if you were not at the helm.

The capital value of a business can be influenced by the number of staff it employs. Some companies are dependent on high staffing levels whilst others get by with a minimum number of workers. In my own firm we have examples of each.

Our advisory business employs consultants to meet clients and understand their needs and support staff to process the back office work. Our asset management company, which invests client money, requires minimal staff as many of the component functions of the business can be contracted out to third parties, thus saving overheads.

Both companies have a capital value, but generally speaking the one that requires the least human involvement is worth more to a prospective purchaser because it will cost less to run and deliver a better return on investment.

All firms are subject to red tape and some sort of compliance to a greater or lesser degree. You'll need to stay ahead of the game and instead of rebelling against regulation, embrace it and work with it. I have witnessed companies that tried to circumvent regulation and it has ended in tears. A prospective buyer will want to be sure your business is 'safe' and has no skeletons in its cupboard.

8. Keep up with the times. If your market is getting smaller, reinvent and adjust.

I mentioned in an earlier chapter the Charles Handy analogy of the frog in the jar of cold water that will not move and will allow itself to be boiled to death when heat is slowly applied to the water. It's not a particularly pleasant image, but illustrates the point that we need to keep abreast of a constantly changing business world or we'll (metaphorically, of course!) perish.

Nothing stays the same. At some point you will need to invigorate or reinvent your company. As a business person you will not operate in isolation, so it would be expected of you to keep up to date with developments in your particular industry and others. You may even become a prime mover in your sector! Personally I try to meet a minimum of three key people in financial services every year and ask them some pretty searching questions about its future, where it's headed and the changes in the pipeline. Based on those conversations, my colleagues and I will adjust our business accordingly.

Successful, old-established companies have always had to reinvent themselves over the years. That's why they still exist today. Nokia and Suzuki are prime examples.

Nokia was originally a 19th century, Finnish, ground wood pulp producer, but moved into various diverse industries including electricity generation, rubber production, paper products and military technology. Today of course, Nokia is known as a major mobile phone manufacturer.

Suzuki originally built weaving looms for Japan's giant silk industry and later for imported cotton. When the cotton market collapsed in 1951, Suzuki seized the opportunity to enter the small motorcycle market in order to satisfy the burgeoning demand for cheap personal transport in post-war Japan. By 1954, the company was producing 6,000 motorcycles a month. The rest, as they say, is history.

9. Be motivated. You're the boss – always be looking for new ideas to improve what you do.

Being the boss is not a 9 to 5 job. It's demanding work. You'll wear many hats and you'll always be wearing one of them, both during and outside normal working hours. You cannot afford to become complacent and lose your motivation.

A solicitors' practice with which I am familiar had a partner who had lost his mojo. He had failed to develop with the business he had actually helped to establish back in the day. He'd simply lost his drive. Whilst his fellow partners and colleagues continued to advance, he became increasingly isolated and disgruntled as he realised no-one valued his opinions any more. His timekeeping 'lapsed' and staff began to question what he did around the place. Difficult though it was, the other partners had to engage him in a frank discussion centred around his future in the business. As it turned out, he had no future in the business and was subsequently 'bought out.' Without the encumbrance, the business became revitalised.

As a motivator, you'll always need to be on the lookout for the next big thing – a scheme or project that will improve your company. Always believe that your best idea is yet to come and be prepared to recognise an opportunity when it presents itself. Don't be put off by others who may not share your drive and insight.

Dan Sullivan of Strategic Coach®, makes a valid point when he says, "Try out your ideas on cheque writers." In other words, test the water with people who would actually *pay* or *invest* in your idea, product or service. If they like it, you're on to a good thing. Have conviction. Stick to your guns.

Michael McIntyre, reportedly the highest grossing comedian in the world in 2012, recently presented a 'pop up' comedy gig at Cheltenham's Everyman Theatre. Here he tested the waters with an audience by recording the bits of his repertoire that got a laugh and ditching the material that didn't!

Here's another personal experience to illustrate the point:

It was 2009. The credit crunch was really starting to bite and everyone was feeling the pinch. Some investment funds had dropped by 30%. My fellow directors and I realised that we needed to do something to help protect our clients' investments in the future. But what?

The answer came rather unexpectedly during a presentation to us by one of the major financial services product providers in London's 'Gherkin' building. We were shown a fund that had weathered the storm rather well and hadn't dropped like a stone during the volatility. It involved employing techniques generally available only to large institutional investors prepared to invest upwards of £1m!

It was time for some serious lateral thinking. I put forward the proposition that as we already administered over £350m of collective client money, could our company (as an entity) not be considered a prospective 'client?' The proposal was favourably received by the product provider, although it had never been 'tried' before, but my colleagues were wary, nervous even, that we were stepping into unknown territory, and could not immediately grasp the bigger picture. But this was a genuine 'light bulb moment' for me and I refused to be put off. And so the journey started.

And what a journey! Three years of hard work and numerous, 'straight talking' negotiations later, our business launched a company, effectively 'sponsoring' two new investment funds with inbuilt volatility protection.

Today, at the time of writing, the funds have some £80m invested in them and over the years have delivered very respectable returns for our clients. As a company in its own right, its capital value (that is, what someone would be prepared to pay to buy the company) is substantial.

I won't pretend it's always easy to drum up the energy and drive to present and convince others of a new idea. You'll meet all kinds of obstacles along the way. But if you have the conviction that you are right, don't be dissuaded.

10. Treat staff well. They need to know they are valued.

We all need to know we are appreciated. Sometimes a sincere 'thank you' or 'well done' is worth more than money in the pocket.

I recall a TV documentary about the space agency, NASA. The presenter was interviewing staff about their roles and he asked one man in particular what he did. The man replied that he was part of the team that put the first man on the moon. Wow. Impressive. It transpired the man was essentially a cleaner, but full marks for the great staff management that had acknowledged and made him feel he was a very important cog in the machinery and definitely 'part of the team.'

All the same, treating staff well involves a little more than showing appreciation. Flexibility and good communications are essential and it has to include the promotion of ongoing development and training and the transfer of skills from an ageing workforce to the young. It has to support employee health and well-being and it has to recognise and adapt to the changing lifestyles of today's workers.

That's what will make your business a great place to work.

11. The right people in the right job. No square pegs in round holes.

In this section, I can do no better than once again give a real-life example to illustrate my point.

I have provided a suite of financial services for an engineering company for more years than I can recall. The current boss, Michael (not his real name), is the son of the founder who sadly passed away. I like to think that my input over the years has helped the company develop.

On one occasion when I visited him, Michael seemed particularly disgruntled and unhappy with his lot. This surprised me somewhat as the £150,000 investment I had made on his behalf over the years was now worth over £500,000 in his pension fund! I asked him what was wrong.

From his office he looked wistfully across the busy shop floor with its whirring lathes, clattering grinding wheels and the smell of lubricant heavy in the air. Then he pointed to the mountain of paperwork on his desk and said, "Look at this stuff. It drives me mad." His secretary piped up and confirmed that Michael felt it incumbent on himself to look at every single piece of post that came in – just like his father had done – instead of leaving it to her.

It was perfectly obvious to me that Michael needed to return to the shop floor where he had initially worked when he joined the firm at 16 years of age. I suggested this to him. I explained that his business had changed beyond all recognition since the early days and he needed to do what he was good at – not what he thought his father would have him do! He was still standing in his father's shadow. He needed to step to one side and create a shadow of his own. He just stared at me.

Twelve months later I visited again. Guess what? Michael was working a CNC machine on the shop floor. He'd gone back to his roots, developed two new successful products and was as happy as a sand boy. The office staff were happier, too!

Michael came over and shook my hand with thanks. He looked 10 years younger than when I had last seen him.

"Well done Michael," I said, "Your father would be proud of you."

12. Persistency wins the prize. Don't be put off your chosen course.

This is simple. If at first you don't succeed then try again... and again, if necessary! To me, 'No' is just a delayed 'Yes.'

Many years ago, when our financial services company's employee benefits proposition was in its infancy, we were asked to tender for the business of a very large, national company. In fact it was the largest enterprise that we had dealt with up to that date.

We were in a 'beauty parade' against 8 of our biggest competitors in the industry and succeeded in being shortlisted. I think it's fair to say our nerves were frayed and we were on tenterhooks during the final presentation. I believed our proposition should have won the day and was disappointed when we did not secure the business. Sometimes big names win the prize, just because they are big names, I remember thinking at the time.

Not to be put off, I phoned the Financial Director of the company for which we'd tendered to find out why we had been unsuccessful. It transpired they simply couldn't make up their minds and decided to start the tender process again!

I then dropped the bombshell – a fact we had included in our presentation but which they had failed to grasp, due, I guess, to fatigue from listening to so many presentations. Their CEO was some £450,000 under insured and I suggested that this oversight needed to be addressed immediately. Due to that fact I suppose that even 'in defeat' I had taken the trouble to reiterate this, the FD immediately asked me to get it sorted.

So, I had succeeded in initiating a relationship which eventually led to my company securing all the business. We still enjoy the partnership to this day.

And I'm pleased to say that my son appears to be following in my footsteps as far as persistency is concerned!

He works for a London-based company, having gained a Degree in Biology. To my amazement and delight he won a top salesman award of an all-expenses-paid, first class trip to Japan. I was immensely proud of course and asked him what he thought made the difference between him and the rest of the salesforce. He said, "I'm not really sure, but I followed up every lead I could and if the prospective client said, 'No, not now, maybe see me later,' I did just that."

13. Market your products and services well. If you don't tell people what you do, how can you expect them to buy from you?

You'll need a web site, whatever the size of your enterprise. If you already have one, keep it fresh. In the modern world, it's the first place people look to check out a company. We all do it. A well-designed site will convey professionalism and can be updated at the click of a mouse. It will also act as a vehicle for news and offers and will allow you to conduct online sales if it fits your business model.

Depending on your type of business, conventional brochures can still be very relevant. There will always be customers who appreciate the look and feel of quality, printed material.

Clearly explain what you do and what customers will get for their money. And don't just do it once. Remind your clients and prospects repeatedly using every means at your disposal. That could include regular company e-bulletins, social media, letters, magazine articles and so on. Advertising may work for you, but it is very expensive and you'll need to design a mechanism to check that you are getting a return on your investment. As a client of mine once said to me, "I know that 50% of my advertising works, but I don't know which 50%!"

Make sure your staff always promote every aspect of your business and ask your satisfied customers to recommend you. Recommendation is the most cost-effective way to promote your business and will deliver the most satisfaction to you.

14. Protect the business. Keep on top of your insurances, legal and tax affairs.

If you are running a successful company you'll need to protect it against all eventualities. Disasters happen to firms every day of the week. Quality insurance is essential of course to cover your premises, machinery, vehicles, IT infrastructure – in fact all the tools of your trade. But what about your most valuable assets – your people? What if anything happens to them? This is where you'll really appreciate the value of professional financial advice because there are products available that will protect your company against the loss of a key person in your organisation or a fellow director, either of which could potentially cause huge disruption to your business – or worse! This is a very big deal in terms of business protection and it's worth paying for the best advice you can afford.

It's also a good idea to make sure your health and safety protocols are in place and up to date, not only to comply with legislation, but to protect your workforce and head off any potential, expensive litigation! And again, depending on the size of your business, you may find a disaster recovery plan would help get you up and running again quickly following, say for example, a flood or fire.

✳✳✳

Helping to run a successful business has been great fun and, yes, profitable. But for me, profit has almost been secondary to the buzz I get from helping clients and thinking up new ideas to push the company further ahead of the curve. As my late, dear father (a man who placed quality above all else in his line of work as a skilled woodworker) used to impress upon me all the time, if a job's worth doing, it's worth doing well.

I can't foresee the day when I'll want to 'retire.' As I think I may have said earlier in this book, why give up doing something you love. I suppose what I'm trying to say really is that having a healthy balance sheet is vital, of course, but part of running a business – any business – should be the exhilaration and satisfaction that making it successful brings.

HEALTHY BUSINESS FINANCES QUICK START TIPS

1. Business should be fun! If you don't enjoy it you are doing something wrong.
2. Follow Richard Branson's advice to budding entrepreneurs: He says that if you have an idea *that's going to make other people's lives better* then you have a business.
3. Make sure your product or service is the best it can be.
4. Listen to your customers.
5. Follow my 14 Principles for Success in Business!

TAILPIECE: INSPIRATION

The story of Kentucky Fried Chicken founder Colonel Harland Sanders is an account of how one man's persistency, motivation, dedication, and ambition, along with hard work, can create success — regardless of age.

At the age of 65, Colonel Sanders had the idea that restaurant owners would love his fried chicken recipe, use it, sales would increase, and he'd get a percentage of it. He drove around the country knocking on doors, sleeping in his car, wearing his white suit. It is reported that he was turned down 1009 times before someone said 'Yes!'

He eventually sold his company for $2m. In 1976, the Colonel was ranked as the world's second most recognizable celebrity.

The moral of my life is don't quit at age 65 — maybe your boat hasn't come in yet. Mine hadn't.

Colonel Harland Sanders

THOUGHT FOR THE DAY: HEALTHY BUSINESS FINANCES

What have I done, or will I do, to improve my business - yesterday / today / tomorrow?

7 HEALTHY RELATIONSHIPS

7 HEALTHY RELATIONSHIPS

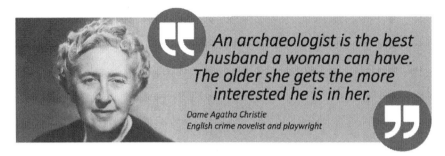

> An archaeologist is the best husband a woman can have. The older she gets the more interested he is in her.
>
> *Dame Agatha Christie*
> *English crime novelist and playwright*

John Donne, the celebrated 17th century English author coined the immortal phrase 'No man is an island, entire in itself,' a sentiment that is as relevant today as it was back then. We all need interactive relationships with others and to a greater or lesser extent, we all depend on one another to lead a happy life.

We want to be happy. Few would disagree with that. But what does 'being happy' actually mean? That's a difficult question because everyone has their own definition of happiness. To some it means having a huge bank balance. To others, simply being able to provide for their family is reward in itself.

We have to decide what happiness means to us as individuals and focus on the conditions that will enable us to achieve it. I believe that whatever brings you happiness, certainly in the long term, will almost certainly depend on healthy relationships with others.

Relationships can take many forms of course and you may already know where you'd prefer to concentrate your efforts, but I'm pretty sure those efforts will be focused on one or more of the following categories:

- Yourself
- Your spouse / partner / potential partner
- Your family
- Your friends
- Work colleagues

- Holidays
- Pets
- The World at large

So let's consider each category in more detail.

Yourself

Whatever other relationships you cultivate, the most important – and often the most overlooked – is the relationship you have with yourself. It is arguably the foundation of everything in your life. Having a sound relationship with yourself improves your ability to nurture relationships with others.

A healthy self-relationship is, above all else, the ability to accept and value yourself as a person and embrace your strengths and weaknesses. Essentially your best friend needs to be yourself. You need to like you!

Self-acceptance is an individual's own awareness of their satisfaction or happiness with themselves. Acceptance of anything does not actually mean resignation. Don't try to be someone that you are not, or try and speak and act in a way that is simply 'not you.' Don't worry what others think, either. Eleanor Roosevelt, America's longest-serving First Lady and wife of former President Franklin D. Roosevelt, said, "You wouldn't worry so much about what others think of you if you realised how seldom they do *(think about you)*."

Personally, I have always tried to adopt the qualities I admire and respect in others to improve myself.

In general terms we are brought up by our parents and teachers to behave within certain set guidelines and standards, so that we can (amongst many other things), find the right job, partner or whatever else we seek in life. But don't we all secretly admire those people we meet who are demonstrably not 'mainstream' but have chosen to lead alternate lives – people who are happy and at one with themselves? The reality is that we are all unique and need to embrace that fact.

Today I count myself fortunate to have many friends, colleagues and clients. But it was not always like that. When I was in my early 20's I moved to London, to seek my fortune – as many did and still do. For a while I was in a very lonely place. I entertained doubts about pretty much everything – including my career path – and this lack of self-confidence lead to negative thinking and a dark time in my life.

This dark time was a whole new experience for me but then a thought occurred to me that turned everything around. I realised that I was the only person I would spend the whole of my life with! So I started to have internal conversations about how I could become stronger in myself and tap into the personal qualities that I liked about myself that would make me happy again. When I accepted all the positive facets that made me who I was, I started a new chapter in my life and was able to move on.

Learning to be happy with who you are doesn't necessarily happen overnight. You'll need to work at it. So I've compiled a few tips that may make it easier for you to cultivate a positive relationship with yourself:

1. **Care for your physical needs:** That includes getting enough sleep and rest, eating sensibly and exercising. Always try to look your best but don't obsess about it.
2. **Be kind to yourself:** 'A little bit of what you fancy does you good.' It could be as simple as a walk in the park, a nice warm bath or relaxing with a good book.
3. **Focus on your inner, mental self:** Ask yourself how you are feeling from time to time. Celebrate your strengths. Don't harbour negative vibes – address them and banish them.
4. **Make time for yourself:** Life may be bedlam around you so go somewhere quiet to think clearly or meditate.
5. **Think of others:** Doing kind and thoughtful things for others makes us all feel good.

Remember that maintaining a positive relationship with yourself is crucial because it's the only relationship you are guaranteed to have every day of your life!

Your spouse / partner / potential partner

When we attended the rehearsal for my eldest daughter's wedding, the Vicar said something very poignant that has stuck with me.

"If you find someone you love, that's amazing. If that love is reciprocated then that is truly awesome and must be one of the greatest things a human being can experience."

Where are you likely to find a partner?

The workplace, dating agencies, online dating websites, singles clubs and holidays – they all have their place and can be very successful, whatever age you are, but they are not for everyone.

You could join a club or society, a walking group or go to places where you can meet like-minded souls that share your interests. You may even meet someone through a mutual friend. And don't forget – animals can be great ice-breakers. You could meet someone walking the dog.

When you do find your perfect partner, you should feel privileged and cherish the relationship every day. It won't all be plain sailing – nothing that delivers high rewards ever is. You'll need to work at it to form a trusting, lasting partnership.

My tips to help maintain a fresh and happy partner relationship are:

Talk to each other: Communication is the glue that holds a relationship together. Be open and honest. Discuss everything. Don't sweep difficult issues under the carpet. Share your feelings.

Show respect and kindness: Your partner is a human being, just like you. He / she will have feelings. Respect them. Don't say hurtful things. Respect your partner's character, time and abilities. Don't try and change who they are.

Share quality time together: It doesn't really matter how much time you spend together as long as that time is quality time. It's fine to share mutual distractions such as lounging on the settee watching TV, but that's not the same as maybe going for a walk together and engaging about the things that matter to you both.

It's OK to be apart, too: Don't live in each other's pockets. Don't stifle each other. Respect each other's independence and give one another space. Trust one another.

Be grateful: You may appreciate your partner, but they won't necessarily know that unless you tell them. Little gifts and tokens — even just well-chosen words — will demonstrate your gratitude for the things they do for you. And appreciate the fact that no-one is perfect. Not even you! Don't focus on your partner's shortcomings.

A loving, physical relationship is very important: But it's not the be-all and end-all of a relationship.

Your family

When I was growing up in the '50s and '60s, a family generally consisted of Mum and Dad, sisters and / or brothers, grandparents, cousins, aunts and uncles. There were kids whose Mums and Dads had sadly died or 'taken off' to pastures new, but these instances were few and far between. Although I probably didn't fully appreciate it at the time, my parents were loving and caring and I had a great up-bringing. I was very lucky and have tried to follow this example with my own children by providing them with as happy a childhood as I could.

The 21st century family comes in all shapes and sizes. There is still the 'traditional' family unit of course, but now we have single parents, same sex parents, 'blended' families — people from different families living together — step parents, divorced parents, adopted or fostered children and just about any combination of the above.

All stages of parenting can be challenging. Once, when my children were young, I was fretting over their futures. A good friend said to me, "Don't worry so much about that. They are really only on loan to us. They are their own people and will travel their own path." Children can be demanding of course, but when they grow into adolescents this can test us to the limit. Tolerance is key. Choose carefully the battles that are worth fighting for.

We all have issues and problems from time to time. It's important to discuss them. Family members are often the first port of call. As my Mum used to say, "A trouble shared is a trouble halved."

I remember during my junior school days hankering after a pair of 'winkle-picker' shoes. You know the sort – the very long, pointed-toed footwear traditionally worn by rock n' roll fans. They were all the rage at the time and I had to have some. My Mum eventually relented and despite dire warnings of lasting foot damage, bought me a pair. Well... my feet hurt, my toes were pinched, I couldn't walk in a straight line and kept tripping myself up. Frankly, I must have looked ridiculous – along with many of my mates!

If you are a parent, I'm sure you'll have had similar confrontations with your own children, as have I, and sometimes, within reason, you just have to let them learn from their own mistakes.

Once again, it's all about keeping the lines of communication open, respecting boundaries and developing mutual trust and respect. The chances are your children will be under similar, or even bigger stresses and strains than you were at their age. Be tolerant, helpful and listen to them. As a good friend suggested to me when we were discussing this very subject – it's not so much that they are *giving* you a hard time, it's more likely they are *having* a hard time and taking it out on you! After all, who else is there to bear the brunt of their anxieties?

Your friends

A good friend of mine bought me a lovely, blue china tea cup for my birthday. I was very pleased, obviously, but genuinely moved when I opened the present and read the inscription on it. 'Friends are the family we choose for ourselves.'

Make no mistake about it. Friends have a huge impact on our happiness. They can help relieve stress, provide comfort and support, prevent loneliness and even strengthen our health. But close friendships just don't happen overnight and it's a fact that many people struggle to meet new friends. Where to begin?

Perhaps not surprisingly, the search for friends is not unlike the search for a potential life partner. A good start would be in the places you frequent – your work or community, for example. Common interests can bring people together as we tend to be drawn to those who like what we like. Hobbies, sport, a shared career path and children can be great ways to meet people.

Many people suffer from a degree of social anxiety. I was once given a tip to help break the ice when I meet new people if I'm not too sure how to start a conversation. It's a little set of questions that show you are interested in someone and allows them to talk, even if they (or you) are relatively shy. And it's a formula that will enable you to find out a great deal about someone from the word 'go.' It's called JIFF – Job, Interests, Family, Future. Ask them questions centred around those four areas. Everyone has something to say on these subjects and you'll be able to respond accordingly. You see, the focus will be on them, not yourself. It will be evident and they'll highly likely be drawn to you more easily.

Be genuine. Show interest. If you are not, it will be apparent and begs the question, why are you bothering in the first place?

Friendships in the main happen naturally. You cannot force them – they are either right or wrong. They are usually forged through common interests.

The key to better friendships is to be a better friend yourself. Give as much – or more – than you receive. Treat your friends as you would wish to be treated. Remember the old saying, 'you get back what you give out?' Try not to have unreasonable expectations.

Finally, research shows that friendships are important to our psychological well-being – friendships bring happiness to our lives. A recent Swedish study found that maintaining a rich network of friends can add significant years to your life.

Work colleagues

We spend 60% of our time in the workplace, which suggests that at times we may see more of our work colleagues than our family! That's a good enough reason to make sure you get along with your fellow workers.

Strong work relationships benefit not only you as an individual, but the organisation itself. It's obvious really, but studies have confirmed that good relationships at work improve morale and lead to greater job satisfaction. Other research shows that healthy work relationships – those that exhibit mutual trust, respect and understanding – actually improve physical health and reduce stress.

Working relationships differ from other relationships because they can exist on a number of levels. On one hand there is the purely professional relationship that enables you do your job better and may improve your career prospects. On the other, there are the personal relationships that exist mainly for social reasons, but at the same time can contribute to workplace satisfaction. Neither are mutually exclusive of course and it's highly likely that if you are engaged in employment, you enjoy both.

And let's not forget that romantic attachments formed in the workplace can and do occasionally, result in marriage.

Holidays

My 'relationship' with the happy holidays I enjoyed as a child are amongst my earliest memories.

Those sort of memories stay with you all your life. Everyone remembers how great it felt at the end of the school summer term with seemingly endless weeks of holiday stretching out ahead. No more homework. No more tests. No more teachers! And yes, the weather did seem infinitely sunnier back then... didn't it?

As an adult I still feel that special sense of anticipation before a holiday. But doesn't everyone? Nowadays the excitement is not borne out of a dislike of work – far from it, I love my work – more the prospect of having extra quality time to spend with my wife, family and friends away from the daily distractions of countless emails, meetings and decision making.

No surprise then that research by long haul travel specialist Kuoni, in conjunction with Nuffield Health, the UK's biggest healthcare charity, has found that holidays are good for you! Of course we would expect a travel operator to say that, but 'getaways' – breaks from the routine of 'normal' everyday life - apparently make you feel better, manage stress, improve sleep patterns, reduce blood pressure, strengthen relationships and may even help you live longer.

Kuoni sent several individuals away abroad on a variety of two week holidays, including touring, volunteer experiences and beach flops. The research reported that, on return, these individuals showed significant upswings in mood and energy levels and felt relaxed with clearer life goals. Blood pressures dropped by an average 6%, sleep quality improved by 17% and resilience to stress improved by a whopping 29%! The benefits in some cases continued for months after the holiday and some even chose to make real change to their lives on return.

A lesson to be learned there, I think, for the estimated 33% of workers who do not take their full holiday entitlement each year. Work is very important – of course it is – but so is taking time to rest and recuperate. You could say that a regular holiday could be regarded as preventative medicine.

Pets
My family has two dogs that sometimes remind us of their presence with a healthy bark at about 2 o'clock in the morning! But I love them really.

So does my wife – she'd have a house full of dogs if she could. I look forward to walking them most days. (The dogs, not the wife!)

It's widely accepted that our relationship with pets has a great influence on our well-being and happiness. Lonely or bereaved souls rely on them for companionship. Disabled people may have hearing or guide dogs. We put our trust in bomb and drug detection dogs to keep us safe.

In much the same way as we benefit from our relationship with pets, they need the relationship with us. They want to feel part of the family. They have emotional needs, too. So we should always be working on improving the bond with our pets. We owe it to them for the pleasure they give us.

The world at large
It is important we see life from a macro point of view as well as from the standpoint of our individual, micro, day-to-day existence.

Our relationship with the world on a political or socio-economic level has a huge influence on us, whether we wish to admit it or not. We are upbeat during prosperous times, but years of austerity and global unrest is enough to make anyone feel down in the dumps. That's understandable, but we have to overcome those low times and regain a positive, happy outlook.

We look back to 'the good old days' when finding employment was easier, everyone still believed in the concept of 'jobs for life,' goods were 'built to last,' shops closed on Sundays and food 'didn't need' preservatives.

Really? Isn't this just rose-tinted hindsight? What about the cold war climate of unease, lower average lifespans and higher infant mortality? The truth is, we may remember the old days as good times because, quite frankly, we survived them and know how they turned out. We rehearse and dwell on good memories and tend to forget the bad stuff.

Conversely we may be anxious about the present and future because we do not know what to expect.

The reality of course is that we are living in the best of times. We have life-enhancing and life-prolonging healthcare which in the main is improving all the time. Most of us would accept that modern technology makes day-to-day living easier and more convenient. We are able to travel the world at the drop of a hat, experiencing everything it has to offer. Generally speaking, we are much better off than our parents and grandparents were, both in terms of health and finances.

Yes, there are serious and horrendous problems in the world today. Each generation has its challenges and it will always be so.

Our values should reflect the past but at the same time they should be firmly rooted in the here and now. If we hope for, or expect perfection, we'll highly likely be sorely disappointed. If we are to achieve a healthy relationship with the world around us we may need to adjust our expectations and be practically realistic. We have to accept that as individuals we can't solve the world's problems, but together we can make tremendous strides forward. I'm a great believer that good will always prevail in the end and we should treat others as we would wish to be treated ourselves.

■■■

So what relationships would you like to work on or improve? Don't forget that sometimes small steps can have a big impact. The following chart is an example compiled from discussions and conversations I have had with people over the years:

YOUR BIGGER FUTURE™ RELATIONSHIP IMPROVER

Which relationship concerns me?	What aspects of it are right or wrong?	How can I improve it?	What outcome will I be happy with?
Myself	I know I am overweight	Get a diet / lifestyle system that I can believe in	Weight loss and more self-esteem
Bob, my work colleague	He is useless and lazy and it's affecting morale in the office	He should leave the company	Harmonious inter-colleague relationships
I am without a partner	I am lonely and want someone to share my life	Join a club that caters for my interests and I may meet someone	Finding a friend that shares my interests

If you'd like to make your own chart, you'll find a blank template at the end of this book or download a copy at www.yourbiggerfuture.co.uk

And finally... another bit of research! Researchers from Brigham Young University in the US have found that people who have lots of close relationships have better odds of living a longer life than those who may be lonely with few friends.

The study, which looked at the lives of some 300,000 people over an average 7½ year period, discovered that strong social connections improve our odds of survival by 50%. Some researchers even felt this figure may be an underestimation! The study went so far as to suggest that low social interaction could have the same effect as being a heavy smoker or alcoholic.

Brigham Young's psychology professor Julianne Holt-Lunstad said that when someone feels a responsibility for another person, or group, the sense of purpose and meaning translates to taking better care of themselves and taking fewer risks.

HEALTHY RELATIONSHIPS QUICK START TIPS

1. Only you can decide what's best for you. Listen to advice from others by all means but make your own decisions
2. Every relationship you cultivate should give you a sense of well-being. If it doesn't, it's not for you. Move on. Complete your personal *Your Bigger Future™ Relationship Improver* chart.
3. A relationship is a two way street. Be prepared to be patient and tolerant.
4. Don't let the sun go down on an argument.
5. Whatever relationships you have, afford them quality time.

TAILPIECE: INSPIRATION

Genetic scientist-turned-Buddhist monk Matthieu Ricard offers up the clearest evidence that a perfect self-relationship can produce extreme happiness. And it's official!

As a young man, Matthieu, 70, was regarded as one of the most promising biologists of his generation, but he forsook his scientific career in 1972 to become a Tibetan Buddhist. His published works include 'The Art of Happiness' and 'The Art of Meditation.'

Matthieu believes that meditation can alter the brain and improve people's happiness in the same way that lifting weights puts on muscle, a theory that seems to have been proved by highly complex MRI scanning of his own brain. The scans showed extraordinarily high levels of upbeat activity and almost invisible levels of negative emotion. He is officially the world's happiest man!

Anyone can be the happiest person in the world if they look for happiness in the right place.

Matthieu Ricard

THOUGHT FOR THE DAY: HEALTHY RELATIONSHIPS

Who and what do I value? Does anything need to change - yesterday / today / tomorrow?

8 SENSE OF PURPOSE

8 SENSE OF PURPOSE

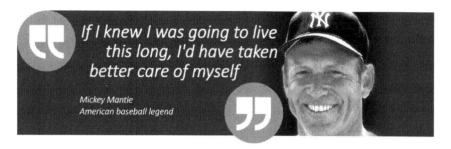

> *If I knew I was going to live this long, I'd have taken better care of myself*
>
> Mickey Mantle
> American baseball legend

It is said that everyone needs to feel like they are contributing to something larger than themselves.

Is that what we recognise as a sense of purpose? I think it is. And if, like me, you consider it to be a fundamental component of a fulfilling life, then you'll agree that a sense of purpose is, or should be, one of the defining characteristics of being human. If our sense of purpose is diminished we are more vulnerable to boredom, anxiety, depression – and in extreme cases – addiction.

Adopting a strong sense of purpose however can exert a very powerful, positive effect. You'll never get up in the morning wondering how to fill your day. Your focus will be crisp and clear, your mind taut and strong and you'll find that life is less complicated and stressful.

Aligning ourselves to a purpose can often make us less self-centred and less focused on our own problems which in turn seem to become less significant. So our sense of wellbeing and self-esteem increases. You may even discover that your true sense of purpose, as a coach or mentor, for example, could be helping others to find theirs. Remember, if you light the way for someone else, you illuminate your own path, too.

Do we inherit a sense of purpose or do we cultivate a purpose in life that is uniquely our own?

I'm not sure we can 'inherit' a purpose in the true sense of the word. However I do think it's true that many individuals adopt and perpetuate the purpose of their parents. Certainly some individuals have a purpose imposed, or inflicted, on them. I'm thinking particularly of those people who have been driven to follow careers or who have been pushed into 'vocations' due to pressure from parents or peers. I would suggest that, clearly, in those instances, the true underlying sense of purpose is weak.

Conversely, a sense of purpose that is *chosen* can be so strong and motivational that it is unshakeable. Apple Inc. co-founder Steve Jobs immediately springs to mind in that respect. That level of purpose usually falls into one or more of four categories:

Accumulative: The attainment of wealth, status and success
Altruistic: Improving the situation of others
Personal development: Gaining knowledge, skills and creativity
Traditional: Religion and sport

These categories are by no means mutually exclusive, can comfortably co-exist or indeed morph, one to another, as life evolves.

The great 19th century industrialist Andrew Carnegie, one of the richest Americans of all time, was driven by a childhood in poverty and the overwhelming sense of purpose to succeed in business. He accumulated fabulous wealth and then became one of, if not the, greatest benefactors the world has ever seen. He believed that 'the man who dies rich, dies disgraced,' and donated nearly 90% of his wealth (the equivalent of $78.6 billion in today's values) to various charities, foundations, libraries and educational institutions.

Oil industry tycoon John D. Rockefeller similarly made an absolute fortune but, allegedly inspired by Carnegie, donated over $500 million to philanthropic causes during his lifetime.

In the modern era, Bill Gates, co-founder of Microsoft, is generally regarded as the richest person in the world today, with an estimated net worth of US $90 billion (as of August 2016). He too has followed the examples of Carnegie and Rockefeller by donating huge amounts of money to various charitable organisations and scientific research programmes via the Bill and Melinda Gates Foundation, the world's wealthiest charitable foundation. It is reported that Bill and Melinda plan to eventually donate 95% of their wealth to charity.

One could argue of course that in the case of all these men, their original, entrepreneurial sense of purpose was a means to an end, in that their true, lifetime sense of purpose was altruistic. Who knows? Interestingly, in context with the theme of this book, both Carnegie and Rockefeller lived to great ages. Rockefeller died at the age of 97!

Research on both sides of the Atlantic suggests that having a strong sense of purpose can add years to your life – regardless of what that purpose may be! The study, published in The Lancet in 2014, was conducted by researchers from UCL, Princeton University and Stony Brook University. It tracked the physical and mental health of more than 9,000 UK adults with an average age of 65 over a period of 8½ years. Researchers discovered that purposeful people were 30% less likely to die during the test period than those with the least sense of wellbeing. Only around 9% of the sample participants in the highest wellbeing category died, compared to 29% of those who had expressed lower purpose in life.

According to another study by Drs. Randy Cohen and Alan Rozanski of Mt. Sinai St. Luke's-Roosevelt Hospital, New York (2015), "Possessing a high sense of purpose in life is associated with a reduced risk of mortality and cardiovascular events."

The results above point to the fact that finding a direction in life and setting over-arching goals for what you want to achieve can actually help you live longer. Part of the reason may be that those with a powerful sense of purpose have more of an incentive to look after their health and are physically fitter.

As I see it, there are four main reasons why purpose has a positive effect on physical and mental well-being and these are:

Motivation: Having a reason for everything we do
Orientation: Knowing where we are and where we're going
Resilience: Overcoming challenges and difficulties
Positivity: Having optimism and hope

The accumulating body of research into sense of purpose across lifespan indicates that it tends to peak during young adulthood, slowly declines throughout middle age and drops sharply in later years. This is a little disturbing because a sense of purpose is arguably more important as we age when it clearly needs to play a key role in promoting well-being and preventing us as older adults from withdrawing socially or feeling detached and superfluous.

I mentioned previously that my mother sadly fell into this category. During most of her life she had always maintained a strong sense of purpose. In her case I believe it was to look after her family and support it to her utmost ability. This motivation sustained her into old age, but gradually, in her late 80s she lost the will and by the time she passed away aged 90, she had literally 'given up.' For my brother and I this was a desperate situation to witness and sadly not an isolated case. I determined that at that age, I still want to be actively engaged in work or a worthwhile project.

I guess that finding a sense of purpose has a lot to do with our mental attitude, cognitive ability and a recognition of our natural talents and personal skills. In other words, we have to determine what we want to do and exactly how we intend to achieve our goals.

There are those individuals of course who had a strong sense of purpose from an early age and there are those who by sheer luck or alignment of the planets, for example, achieved wealth and fame without any sense of purpose whatsoever. And then there are those people, like me, who have to work at it, who have to put a plan in place to achieve a desired goal.

Without wishing to continually repeat myself (but I will because it's important), the key element is to find out what we really enjoy doing, what we are good at, and build on our strengths. Only then, I believe, will our true sense of purpose manifest itself. We need to identify our personal skills and then work to develop them.

For as long as I can remember, I have enjoyed athletic sport and during my school days was good at the long jump. But I was rubbish at the high jump. I knew I'd never be any good at it. Nevertheless, my old sports master encouraged me to persevere with the high jump in an effort to improve. Well, guess what. I never really got any better. Then later, the truth dawned on me. Would it not have made more sense to work harder on the long jump, where I showed great potential and have become (maybe!) a champ, than waste time on something at which I knew deep down I'd only ever be mediocre? As Dan Sullivan, founder of the Strategic Coach® Program once told me, "If you work throughout your life on improving your weaknesses, what you'll get are a lot of really strong weaknesses."

But what is it about us that makes us take the actions we take? How can we understand our strengths and apply them to the things we care about and in so doing create our individual sense of purpose? Very often these qualities are innate, maybe even subliminal, but are the parts of us that drive our success. There is a way you can discover the skills hidden inside you. It's the way I discovered my innate abilities. It's called the Kolbe A Index (www.kolbe.com). Kolbe is a company that helps people of all ages to identify their instinctive talents, develop their confidence, and use their innate abilities to succeed in a plethora of situations. There is a modest charge, but look on it as an investment in yourself. It will give you new direction and boost your confidence. You'll highly likely discover 'hard wired' skills you never knew you possessed.

I talk a lot about personal skills and Kolbe is certainly one way to discover yours. But there is another way which I was taught many years ago during an entrepreneurial coaching workshop in Toronto, Canada. Here's how it works:

In life there are activities at which you will be well below average. There are activities at which you will be about average. There are activities at which you'll be reasonable and then there will be those at which you really excel. So during the course of a week or a month, make a note of all the activities in which you engage and divide them into those four categories. You may be very surprised. I was. You may, like me, discover that the vast majority of your time is spent on 'below average' or 'average' activities.

To complete this exercise, you now need third party intervention to gain a complete, balanced result. Write to, or email, 12 people that you know you can count on for an honest response. *(In my case, to achieve a balance, I asked three family members, three friends, three work colleagues and three business clients.)* Explain the reason for the request and then ask them what they think you are good at, what they consider to be your personal skills, talents, abilities, characteristics, and personality traits. Ask them to be honest, not diplomatic! Note that you are not asking people what you are *not* good at. This is about developing more of an understanding of what you are already good at and could maybe improve even more. The feedback may, or may not be flattering, but it will certainly be interesting. You'll learn things about yourself that could surprise you. Significantly, it should help you recognise those skills that make you who you are, or what you could become. The skills that you need to identify your sense of purpose.

As always, I found it helpful to devise a chart that would help me encapsulate my thought processes and concentrate the mind. This is how I pinned down *my* personal skills to identify *my* true Lifetime Sense of Purpose.

This is a copy of my personal chart:

YOUR BIGGER FUTURE™ LIFETIME SENSE OF PURPOSE

How to recognise your Personal Skills

1. What are the activities that you enjoy and love?	I like helping people
	I enjoy my job that allows me to help improve the lives of others
	I am pleased that I am respected enough that clients refer me to others
	I enjoy being fit enough to enjoy sport, leisure activities and holidays
	I love spending time with family and friends
	I enjoy new experiences
2. List your qualities and abilities as identified by others	'Sees the 'bigger picture' and always looking to develop his company'
	'Safe pair of hands and fun to work with - a 'people person''
	'Good communicator that understands people's needs'
	'Professional, fair, believes all parties should gain in business'
	'Genuine, selfless person - the real deal!'
	'Can always be relied upon - always does what he says he will'
3. Distill the elements from 1. and 2. above and extract key words	Helping people, improving lives
	Seeing the 'bigger picture'
	Developing company
	Good communication skills
	Understands people's needs
	Professional, fair and reliable
4. Use those key words to identify your Personal Skills	I am able to connect with people and strategise viable solutions to help them. This in turn creates opportunities for their, mine and my company's future well-being
5. Refine your Personal Skills into your basic Sense of Purpose	Connecting with people to help them improve their lives
6. Refine further into a description that truly sums up your Lifetime Sense of Purpose	"Communicating with people and delivering solutions for them which will improve their positions and will help them develop to their full potential"

(A blank template can be found at the end of this book or downloaded from www.yourbiggerfuture.co.uk)

I felt liberated by the exercise. I was able to establish my sense of purpose, which in essence, in my case, could also be regarded as my lifetime job description.

It's all about making yourself a better 'you.' It's about finding your passion in life – the force that drives you – and then applying it.

There are many other factors in addition to personal skills that will contribute to, and influence, your sense of purpose. For example, consider the word 'retirement.' It invariably has a different meaning depending on with whom you are discussing the subject. To some, obviously, it means an 'escape' from the workplace and freedom to pursue another way of life and new adventures. Others may regard retirement as a reward for a long, happy and fruitful career, happy with the prospect of having enough money not to need to work any longer. Then there will be those who may be resentful at having to leave a situation that they've come to love or rely on, fearful for a future that seems to be empty and offer no substitute.

When I'm asked about retirement, my reply is always the same. "Why would I want to retire and leave behind things I enjoy doing?" As I see it, you should only 'retire' from those things you do not relish. Many retire from work to enjoy the freedom to indulge hobbies and spend more time with family and friends. Good luck to them. However, quite often, this sense of freedom does not last and gives way to a need to get back to doing something meaningful and purposeful. It is one thing to retire from a career and occupation, but 'retiring from life' is an entirely different proposition.

During our lifetime we accumulate a vast amount of knowledge, experience and confidence. Call it 'wisdom.' All too often, when people retire, this wisdom is lost to society and with it one's sense of purpose. Some regret the loss of status and the feeling of being 'somebody.' How sad is that? The late, great English comedian Eric Morecambe encapsulated that feeling when he said, "Sometimes it worries me. I feel something's got to give. I know what Harry Secombe *(the late, Welsh comic genius)* meant when he said he's worried that one day, the phone will ring and a mystic voice will say, 'Thank you Mr. Secombe. Now can we have it all back?' "

We all need to know we're wanted and valued – for all of our lives. The feeling that others still need our wisdom, opinions and guidance. The feeling that we can still be of use, that we can still help others and make a difference.

Aligning yourself to a charity, for example, could fulfil your sense of purpose and satisfy a need to contribute to the greater good of society. In my company, we have a charitable foundation called *Heartfelt,* which raises money for many worthy causes. Staff and I take part in fund-raising events that stretch our abilities but from which we ultimately gain a huge amount of satisfaction and achievement. We created a blog in 2015 which followed our fundraising progress during the year. It is still online at www.brian60.co.uk if you'd like to take a look. But the real point I want to make is this: When we hand over the funds raised to the various charities, very often the charity representatives or 'ambassadors,' will be retired people who have made it their mission in life – possibly their renewed sense of purpose – to help others less fortunate than them.

A very good friend of mine and a source of great inspiration to me for many years, said to me shortly before he passed away, "Life. It's about leaving it better than you found it." I can think of no better way to illustrate why having a sense of purpose is so important for us all – for all of our lives.

SENSE OF PURPOSE QUICK START TIPS

1. Decide what gives you the greatest satisfaction in life. The chances are that will be your sense of purpose.
2. Ask others what they consider to be your best qualities and skills.
3. Recognise those skills – they make you who you are and who you could become. Complete your personal *Your Bigger Future™ Lifetime Sense of Purpose* chart.
4. Perhaps align yourself to a cause for which you have a great passion.
5. Make sure your purpose makes you feel wanted and valued.

TAILPIECE: INSPIRATION

Anna Turney is a British Paralympic Skier. She was one of the UK's brightest snowboarding hopes when an accident left the then 26 year old paralysed from the waist down.

Determined not to be defeated and despite being told she'd never take part in competitive sport again, Anna was determined to get back to the mountains. She took up monoskiing and within three years was chosen to represent GB at the 2014 Vancouver Paralympics.

Now a motivational speaker and working with various high profile charities, Anna continues to inspire others.

 Think positive and great things happen.

Anna Turney

THOUGHT FOR THE DAY: SENSE OF PURPOSE

Who did I, or will I, help to have a better day - yesterday / today / tomorrow?

9 FUN ALONG THE WAY

9 FUN ALONG THE WAY

> *Fun is at the core of the way I like to do business and it has been the key to everything I've done from the outset.*
>
> Sir Richard Branson
> English business magnate, investor and philanthropist

Most of us experience it from time to time. The thought that maybe, sometimes, life is just a little bit... well... boring.

You know the feeling. Life suddenly feels pretty mundane and full of routine. You tend to eat the same thing for your breakfast every day. If you have a job, you take the same route to work – at exactly the same time – five days a week. You probably alternate between the same few sets of clothes and shoes. If you are a fan of social media you'll constantly come across people that seem to be living a more exciting life than you. OK, you will have your own moments of fun and joy but even these moments can become predictable with repetition. Does that sound familiar?

Depending on your age, you may be reading this and thinking, 'That's not me. I'm having fun.' And if you are in your twenties, for example, that's probably true. The world is your oyster. You have energy and hopefully, good health. You don't have too many responsibilities. You may have landed a job with exciting prospects. You can still feel pretty good even after a night on the town. (But – as we are all too well aware – even younger people can suffer from angst and the feelings of inadequacy.) Fast forward a few years to life's realities of family, mortgage, work pressures and so on and you may find that your mojo is not what it was.

We are creatures of habit. Although often boring, our routines are comfortable. The safe option. Whilst we may crave a little excitement in our lives, the thought of doing something about it can be quite daunting.

But if you always do what you've always done, you'll always get what you've always got. Which is fine of course, if you are happy with that situation. It does, after all, provide a sense of being in control, security and 'belonging.'

A definition that I read recently described 'fun' as 'something that provides mirth or amusement which is usually doubled when shared with someone else.' I equate fun with happiness. I look around and observe people who are clearly not enjoying their lives. Some appear to be born pessimists, resigned to being unhappy and the feeling that life has dealt them a few curved balls or cruel blows. Perhaps they have not achieved what they wanted in life. Perhaps they believe that 'having fun' is frivolous and superficial. Or perhaps they think it is a misplaced priority, bearing in mind the bad news that is served up to us daily by the media.

I take a different view. It's clear to me that getting depressed about the problems of the world never did anyone any good. I believe that having fun, getting away from work concerns, having a laugh, doing something joyous and yes – even a little frivolous on occasions – can reduce stress, enhance creativity, rebuild energy levels and improve relationships. And it can help restore lost mojos!

I suppose in a way this harks back to everything I've already talked about in this book. That if we address what we hope to accomplish in life, strive to be fit in mind and body, cement relationships and cultivate our sense of purpose, then we will be well on the way to creating the basis for long term fun and enjoyment as the backbone of our day to day lives. Having fun will once again become an intrinsic part of our psyche. I say 'once again,' because each of us is born with a propensity to have fun and most of us, I hope, remember our childhoods as happy, fun-filled times.

In my experience, people who achieve great things in life have had fun achieving them. Having fun is not a diversion from a successful life – it can be the pathway to it.

We can all find inspiration around us. We have a family friend who inspires everyone with whom he comes into contact. He is an RAF Korean

War veteran and recently accomplished a wing walk to celebrate his 85th birthday. On landing, his first words were, "Can I do that again?" He lives alone, his wife having sadly passed away many years ago as a result of Motor Neurone Disease. He has experienced some terrible tragedies during his lifetime. But he keeps himself fit and busy and derives great pleasure from helping friends and neighbours with their household problems. Quite frankly, he has energy that would put many 20 year olds to shame.

How does he manage it? Well clearly he still has a great sense of purpose in that he enjoys helping others. He keeps himself fit and healthy and has his life experiences in the forces to draw upon.

To bring the fun back you need to break out of your comfort zone. You don't have to do anything drastic to introduce more interests and excitement into your life. Small and simple changes, just a shift in your thinking, can shake up your world enough to make it more fun, fascinating, adventurous and yes, healthier, too.

But don't just take my word for it. Research carried out in 2009 by Psychology Professor Sarah D. Pressman of the University of California and her colleagues, shows that taking time out and engaging in pleasurable activities leads to both psychological and physical well-being. Professor Pressman reported that these enjoyable activities have a beneficial effect on coping and restoration, particularly during stressful times.

Participants in the study, which measured the time they spent on fun activities against their psychological well-being, blood pressure, stress and hormone levels, reported greater experience of positive emotions, life satisfaction and engagement, lower depression scores, lower blood pressure and improved physical function. The research also confirmed that engaging in pleasurable leisure activities acts as a 'stress buffer.' To me this clearly indicates that you really can take care of yourself by having fun!

Throughout my life I have made every effort to balance my work and lifestyle to make room for the fun times.

Many years ago, a friend inspired me to take up his sport – Karate. I obtained my black belt after just six years and persevered and trained for 17 years. I taught the sport for ten years, had trials for the England B Squad and even fought the Spanish Champion in Tenerife. I felt good, confident, competitive and fit. Whilst I had always run for fitness purposes, I later raised my game and completed the London Marathon twice for charitable causes.

Those were fun and exciting times and I believe the discipline required to train instilled in me life lessons that helped me throughout my career to date.

When I reached my 60th birthday, I decided to mark the occasion by setting myself six challenges. The challenges coincided with a fund-raising charity year in my place of work and would help raise money for the cause, draw in others to help, support and participate and of course be great fun – if a little scary and dare I say, dangerous.

I elected to:
- Run a half marathon
- Undertake The Three Peaks Challenge
- 'Fly' the monster, 100mph zip wire in North Wales
- Experience a wing walk
- Learn to ski and attempt a 'black run'
- Write a book

With the publication of this book I have achieved the six challenges. They were all fun (albeit, some more than others!). With the help of many friends, family and colleagues, we raised over £ 17,000 for charity.

You can read all about my experiences on my blog www.brian60.co.uk .

It had also been a dream of my brother and I to ride American Route 66 on Harley Davidson motorcycles. We'd harboured this ambition since our teenage years, tearing around the countryside on our old bikes. It seemed to us the ultimate fun thing to do on motorbikes and in 2007 we realised our dream. We had such a great time we did it again in 2016 – the second time to celebrate the 90th anniversary of the inauguration of the road in 1926. A great bonus for us was that on the second occasion we were accompanied by TV's Travel Channel presenter and film producer, Henry Cole (www.henrycole.tv). We met some amazing people, rode over 2,600 miles across 8 states and 3 time zones and experienced every type of weather known to man. Was it fun? Absolutely! It was also an achievement because it stretched our limits of endurance and concentrated the mind like nothing else.

I realise that not everyone may wish to ride a bike across America to get fun out of life! It's all about what you consider fun – on your own terms.

So if your life has started to become a tad boring and stale, maybe it's time to do something about it. It's not as complicated or difficult as you may think, but only you know what 'having fun' means to you. Don't try to copy someone else's idea of fun if, deep down, it's not right for you. Because where is the fun in that? Fun and excitement is relative to your individual personality and circumstances.

I could suggest hundreds of ways to have fun, some of which may appeal to you, some of which you may not relish at all. But it would be remiss of me if I didn't put forward a few basic ideas that you could consider to get started on your quest for fun.

1. **Clear some space:** Get rid of, or delegate, some of the clutter in your life to make room for fun and excitement.
2. **Plan a trip:** Even if you can't afford it right now, just researching, planning and dreaming can give you a boost and build excitement.
3. **Learn something new:** Take up a hobby and / or attend some classes. You'll meet new people who share your interests and who knows where that might lead...
4. **Change your car:** Get something more exciting, or at least take a test drive behind the wheel of your dream car.

5. **Do that one big thing:** Something that may have been in your mind for some time – maybe a job change, a house move, a new relationship. Take the first step because this will create the momentum to take you further.

These are relatively short term goals. Why not take time out to plan your 'bucket list' – the things you want to experience or achieve during your lifetime. This is all part of the preparation for Your Bigger Future™. If we are likely to live that much longer, our bucket lists can be longer too. As an example, this is my latest, updated list.

YOUR BIGGER FUTURE™ BUCKET LIST

An experience I hope to have during my lifetime	Why I want to do this	What I will gain from this experience	Action needed to make possible
Visit Australia and New Zealand	We have family there and friends	Meet family again and explore the two countries	Start planning and allocate funds
Take the whole family to Disneyland / Universal Studios	Legendary holiday destination for all	We can all enjoy being children again!	Start planning and allocate funds
Another long-haul motorcycle trip, (possibly Europe) with brother and friends	Route 66 was an amazing experience and I want to do something similar again	It will be great fun shared with other like-minded enthusiasts	Decide a route and plan it
Fundraising for charities that have a personal connection	Because charities will always need money	The satisfaction of helping others less fortunate	Set aside time to plan strategy with key people

If you'd like to make your own list, you'll find a blank template at the end of this book or download a copy at www.yourbiggerfuture.co.uk

HAVING FUN QUICK START TIPS

1. Don't be afraid to step outside your comfort zone.
2. Life may not be perfect, but count your own blessings.
3. Make room in your life for fun and share the good times with others.
4. Be frivolous once in a while.
5. Plan ahead for all the fun things you want to do in the future and complete a personal *Your Bigger Future™ Bucket List* chart.

I'd like to close this chapter with perhaps one of the most inspirational stories you are ever likely to hear. It is the story of a man born with a disability that meant all the odds were stacked against him from the word go. Read this and you'll believe anything is possible.

TAILPIECE: INSPIRATION

Australian-born Nick Vujicic was born with phocomelia, a rare disorder characterised by the absence of arms and legs. Despite being limbless – missing both arms at shoulder level, no legs and just one small foot with two toes protruding from his left thigh – he can surf, swim, play golf and football.

Nick graduated from college at the age of 21 with a double major in Accounting and Financial Planning. After overcoming bullying, ignorance and discrimination, he realised his true mission in life: to use his disability to start conversations that change lives. He became a motivational speaker with a focus on hope and finding meaning in life.

He has spoken over 3,000 times in more than 57 countries, inspiring positive change, persistence and determination. His core message is that no matter what your circumstances, you can overcome almost anything.

Nick has written a number of related books. You can watch him in action at
https://www.youtube.com/watch?v=J6I266-JNpo

He is married with two sons and currently lives in California.

 I'm happy. Why aren't you?

Nick Vujicic

THOUGHT FOR THE DAY: FUN ALONG THE WAY

What was a fun activity yesterday? What will be fun today / tomorrow?

10 USEFUL TEMPLATES

10 USEFUL TEMPLATES

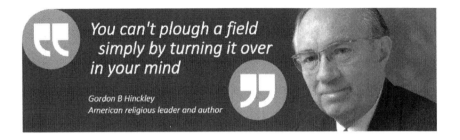

You can't plough a field simply by turning it over in your mind

Gordon B Hinckley
American religious leader and author

Karl Pearson, the influential English mathematician, once famously proposed, 'That which is measured improves. That which is measured *and reported* improves exponentially.'

If you have ever kept a chart to 'track' or improve your progress or performance in a particular area, you'll realise that this statement is true. 'Trackers' tend to go to enormous lengths to improve those things they measure, sometimes almost subconsciously.

As you will have noticed throughout this book, I am a great believer in progress charts – because they do work for me. I find that committing my goals and projects to paper, or in a computerised format, helps solidify my ideas and concepts and acts as a visual reminder of certain activities in which, for example, my performance or life can be improved.

I hope then that you found my charts inspiring. In the following pages you'll find blank template versions that you can use to track your personal projects and progress. Alternatively, you can download them from www.mybiggerfuture.co.uk , complete them 'on screen' and / or print out as many copies as you like.

I'm sure you'll find the charts useful in helping you to focus on those areas of your life that you feel could be improved on your journey towards Your Bigger Future™.

YOUR BIGGER FUTURE™ HEALTHY BODY NUMBERS

Start date:	STARTING NUMBERS	TARGET NUMBERS	TARGET DATE	MONTH 1	MONTH 3	MONTH 6
Weight						
Body mass index (BMI)						
Body fat						
Abdominal / Visceral fat						
Blood pressure						
Cholesterol						

YOUR BIGGER FUTURE™ ACHIEVABLE GOALS

THIS QUARTER'S GOALS	1 YEAR GOALS	3 YEAR GOALS	LIFETIME GOALS
Family and friends			
Work and financial			
Fitness and health			
Wild card things!			

YOUR BIGGER FUTURE™ CONFIDENCE BOOSTER

What gives me confidence?

1

2

3

4

5

6

7

8

9

10

YOUR BIGGER FUTURE™ HABIT ADJUSTER

CATEGORY	MY CURRENT HABITS	HOW I CAN IMPROVE THIS HABIT?
Healthy body		
Healthy mind		
Healthy finances		
Healthy relationships		
Healthy sense of purpose		
Having fun		

YOUR BIGGER FUTURE ™ JOURNAL

PHYSICAL HEALTH
What have I done, or will I do, to improve or maintain my health - yesterday / today / tomorrow?

Yesterday	
Today	
Tomorrow	

MENTAL HEALTH
What have I done, or will I do, to boost my confidence - yesterday / today / tomorrow?

Yesterday	
Today	
Tomorrow	

PERSONAL MONEY
What have I done, or will I do, to make or save money - yesterday / today / tomorrow?

Yesterday	
Today	
Tomorrow	

BUSINESS MONEY
What have I done, or will I do, to improve my business - yesterday / today / tomorrow?

Yesterday	
Today	
Tomorrow	

RELATIONSHIPS
Who and what do I value? Does anything need to change - yesterday / today / tomorrow?

Yesterday	
Today	
Tomorrow	

SENSE OF PURPOSE
Who did I, or will I, help to have a better day - yesterday / today / tomorrow?

Yesterday	
Today	
Tomorrow	

HAVING FUN
What was a fun activity yesterday? What will be fun today / tomorrow?

Yesterday	
Today	
Tomorrow	

YOUR BIGGER FUTURE™ PLANNED EXPENDITURE

TIME FRAME	EVENT	AMOUNT NEEDED	DATE NEEDED	HOW FUNDED	NOTES
Short Term *					
Medium Term**					
Long Term***					

* Short Term: 1 - 2 years   ** Medium Term: 2 - 10 years   *** Long Term: 10 years +

YOUR BIGGER FUTURE™ PERSONAL FINANCES

INCOME	ALLOCATION
$\frac{1}{3}$	**Financial goals**
$\frac{1}{3}$	**Fixed costs**
$\frac{1}{3}$	**Flexible spending**

YOUR BIGGER FUTURE™ 'SWOT'

STRENGTHS	WEAKNESSES	OPPORTUNITIES	THREATS

YOUR BIGGER FUTURE™ RELATIONSHIP IMPROVER

Which relationship concerns me?	What aspects of it are right or wrong?	How can I improve it?	What outcome will I be happy with?

YOUR BIGGER FUTURE™ LIFETIME SENSE OF PURPOSE

How to recognise your Personal Skills

1. What are the activities that you enjoy and love?	
2. List your qualities and abilities as identified by others	
3. Distill the elements from 1. and 2. above and extract key words	
4. Use those key words to identify your Personal Skills	
5. Refine your Personal Skills into your basic Sense of Purpose	
6. Refine further into a description that truly sums up your Lifetime Sense of Purpose	

YOUR BIGGER FUTURE™ BUCKET LIST

An experience I hope to have during my lifetime	Why I want to do this	What I will gain from this experience	Action needed to make possible

YOUR BIGGER FUTURE™ NOTES

11 SUMMARY AND CREDITS

11 SUMMARY AND CREDITS

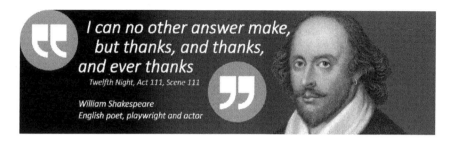

I can no other answer make, but thanks, and thanks, and ever thanks

Twelfth Night, Act 111, Scene 111

William Shakespeare
English poet, playwright and actor

Nothing beats life experiences to advance the scope of human knowledge and understanding.

I've certainly drawn on my life's experiences to date during the preparation of this book, but at the same time I've also undergone a pretty steep learning curve as I've developed a greater appreciation of what it really means to have it within our own power to enjoy a much healthier, wealthier, happier, longer life than we could have imagined just a few short years ago.

I've attempted to leave no stone unturned in finding out how we can make the most of the lives we have now and the longer lives we and our children can hopefully look forward to in the future.

At the beginning of the journey, I explained why I'm convinced that a Calorie Controlled Lifestyle is the bedrock of good health and why good health is the cornerstone of longevity. I remain convinced that this is true. But good health is not enough in itself, I'm also sure of that. Having enough money is important and so is the support of family and friends, but at the end of the day it is our sense of purpose and happiness that will define our lives.

It's been a long, fascinating journey, but like all great journeys I haven't done it alone. I've been able to draw on advice and encouragement from family, friends, colleagues and clients, not to mention casual acquaintances. All have gone out of their way to express an interest in what is fast becoming *the* great topic of conversation of our age - how we really can all look forward to an extended, quality lifestyle – as long as we have our wits about us and the self-will to follow a few, relatively simple guidelines.

It's just not possible to thank everyone, but I'd like to mention in particular Dan Sullivan and his colleagues at Strategic Coach®, including Russell Schmidt, to whom I am indebted for over 20 years of solid, thought-provoking and life-changing advice.

Dr. Michael Mosley, of course, seriously opened my eyes to the benefits of a Calorie Controlled Lifestyle and this has to have been one of the defining moments of my life. Similarly, gerontologist Aubrey de Grey's theories about the extension of human life form the very cornerstone of this book.

And where would we be without the research teams throughout the world who work tirelessly to advance and contribute to our thinking and experiences.

I am therefore indebted to the following:

Dan Sullivan: Strategic Coach®
https://www.strategiccoach.com/

Dr. Michael Mosely:
http://www.bbc.co.uk/iplayer/episode/b01lxyzc/horizon-20122013-3-eat-fast-and-live-longer
The Fast Diet by Dr. Michael Mosley and Mimi Spencer

Dr. Aubrey de Grey:
https://www.ted.com/talks/aubrey_de_grey_says_we_can_avoid_aging
Ending Aging: The Rejuvenation Breakthroughs That Could Reverse Human Aging in Our Lifetime by Aubrey de Grey, with Michael Rae

Laura Germine / Joshua Hartshorne:
http://lauragermine.org/articles/psychsci2015.pdf

Welma Stonehouse:
https://www.ncbi.nlm.nih.gov/pmc/articles/PMC4113767/
http://www.nzherald.co.nz/lifestyle/news/article.cfm?c_id=6&objectid=1
0823174

Dr. Madhav Thambisetty:
http://www.sciencetimes.com/articles/7273/20150907/link-between-
obesity-and-alzheimers-discovered-study.htm

Miscellaneous:
http://jamanetwork.com/journals/jamainternalmedicine/article-
abstract/2587081

http://news.ubc.ca/2015/07/23/aerobic-exercise-is-as-good-for-the-
older-brain-as-it-is-for-the-body/

http://www.sleephealthjournal.org/article/S2352-7218%2815%2900015-
7/fulltext

https://www.lv.com/adviser/news/cost-of-care-exceeds-average-
pension-pot

http://www.resolutionfoundation.org/media/press-releases/millennials-
facing-generational-pay-penalty-as-their-earnings-fall-8000-behind-
during-their-20s/

http://www.royallondon.com/about/media/news/2016/february/new-
report-highlights-the-death-of-retirement/

http://www.health.harvard.edu/newsletter_article/the-health-benefits-
of-strong-relationships

http://www.kuoni.co.uk/holiday-health-experiment

https://news.byu.edu/news/prescription-living-longer-spend-less-time-
alone

www.kolbe.com

https://www.sciencedaily.com/releases/2015/12/151203112844.htm

https://www.ncbi.nlm.nih.gov/pmc/articles/PMC2863117/

Finally, a big thank you to all those celebrities, past and present, who have provided the amusing and insightful quotations, to my wife Deb for her encouragement, patience and support and to my brother Dave for his tireless help in writing and designing this book.

70938948R00098

Made in the USA
Columbia, SC
20 May 2017